Numerology

GEDDES & GROSSET

This edition published 1999 by Geddes & Grosset
Reprinted 2002

© 1997 Geddes and Grosset,
David Dale House, New Lanark, ML11 9DJ, Scotland

Cover photograph by Sarah Jones courtesy of the
Telegraph Colour Library

ISBN 1 85534 289 8

Printed and bound in the UK

Contents

Introduction

Numerology is the name given to an ancient method of studying numbers that has been in use for thousands of years. It is used to give insight into people's personalities and their motivation in life. It is an ancient science that is used to analyse people's characters.

The most popular form of numerology in use today is based on the work of Pythagoras, the famous Greek mathematician and philosopher who lived during the sixth century bc. This book employs a system which is based on the work of Pythagoras.

It was Pythagoras's belief that numbers were the first of all things in nature. It was his belief that numbers were the basis of everything, in the natural, spiritual and scientific world. He believed that everything could be reduced to mathematical terms and that everything had a numerical value. Through studying the world in numerical form, he sought to achieve greater understanding of the world he lived in. Pythagoras, who believed that numbers created order and beauty, founded a school for students to follow his philosophy, and this was known as the Italic or Pythagorean School.

The Pythagoreans believed that numbers could represent religious and holy things, for example, one represented unity (and therefore God), two was duality (the Devil), and four was a sacred and holy number on which they could swear oaths. Numbers were also thought to represent the planets and elements: one represented the sun, two stood for the moon, five was fire, six stood for the earth and eight represented the air.

Pythagoras formulated the concept called the Music of the Spheres', based on the idea that all the planets in the universe formed a harmonious whole consisting of a musical chorus. He discovered that there was a relationship between sound and numbers, and developed this discovery to form his metaphysical concept. He suggested that every planet was a certain distance from a central point in the universe and that if an invisible string connected each planet to the central point, when plucked the string would emit a certain tone or vibration. Each sound or vibration could be associated with a particular number. He also believed that the sound or vibration of the universe dictated by the position of the planets would have a strong influence on the character of an individual born at that particular time.

Numerologists believe that the numbers one to nine have specific characteristics, and these characteristics are the basis for the methods of analysis described in this book. The numbers one to nine are the only numbers that are believed to be significant to numerology. All numbers greater than nine can be reduced to a single digit by the process of fadic addition, for example:

12 is reduced to 3 by adding 1 and 2;

49 is reduced to 4 by adding 4 and 9 which equals 13 and subsequently adding 1 and 3 to make 4.

The numbers one to nine have different characteristics and therefore different influences on the characters and personalities of individuals. The influences of the numbers one to nine are examined in the following chapters. Each number is different. No one number is better or worse than any other. They are simply different.

Numerologists believe that through studying your date of birth and your name it is possiblle to analyse your character. They believe that it is possible to identify the potential that exists within you, your motivation, the way you interact with other people and the main characteristics asscociated with your date of birth and name.

By studying your personality through numerology, numerologists believe that it is possible to know yourself better, learn to accept yourself for who you are and modify your behaviour where appropriate. There is a chapter devoted to the analysis of the compatibility of the different birth date numbers. It does not necessarily follow that if the partner you are with has an apparently incompatible birth date number that the relationship an impossible one. The comparison highlights the points of difference where there should be compromise on both parts. You should not try to change yourself but be aware of all the aspects of your character and learn to live with them.

Birth Date Numbers

Your birthday holds the key to the most significant number in your life. By doing a simple mathematical calculation it is possible to find your birth date number. This number will be in the range of 1 to 9. The basis of numerology is that there are essentially nine personality types dictated by birth dates. In terms of numerology, everyone fits into one of these nine types.

Later in this chapter you will find a breakdown of each of the nine personality types. The descriptions of the personality types will give you an insight into how your birth date influences your relationships, your career and your leisure interests, as well as providing a general overview of the main characteristics associated with that birth date number. Also included are lists of famous people who share that birth date number and colours that are beneficial to incorporate in your life.

You may find that in reading about your birth date number and its associated characteristics you are already aware of having many of the traits listed or you may find little similarity between the description and your perception of yourself. Everyone is obviously an individual and people are all different, so it would not be possible to classify all the people in the world into nine types with no variances. It may be that you are not typical of your birth date number or that the influences of numerology are not particularly strong in your life.

However, this can be a starting point for a journey of self-discovery and an opportunity to get to know yourself really well. It is possible you have potential that you have not explored or aspects of your character that you have dismissed or tried to ignore.

It is important to be aware of all the aspects of your personality, not just the positive ones. If you have a tendency to be self-centred then it is important to recognize this and to learn to accommodate this aspect of your character.

If in reading about your birth date number personality you read about a characteristic that you find unappealing, do not instantly deny that you have that particular trait or that numerology has no significance for you. It is difficult to accept that we all have characteristics of which we are less than proud, but to know yourself fully you have to be aware of your true self. Negative characteristics exist in everyone— no one is infallible, and this is important to remember. It would be wrong to try to change your personality and rid yourself of imperfections. Once you are aware of yourself and your negative characteristics, you can monitor them and keep them in check. It is important not to let your negative characteristics dominate or let them create unhappiness for others.

In your journey of self-knowledge modesty has no place. If you have a special talent or gift, acknowledge it and consider how you can develop it. It is important to be comfortable with yourself and to allow yourself to appreciate your finer points.

Your birth date number personality type does not necessarily indicate existing characteristics but those that you may potentially have as a result of your birth date. You may find that, for example, in reading about your birth date number that your personality type is confident and assertive but that you do not feel that this is the case for you. In discovering your true self it is sometimes helpful to get input from other people. It could be that others consider you to be full of confidence and brimming with assertiveness. If you find that others share your view, examine why you are lacking confidence—is there something that you can do to feel more in control. Try experimenting with assertiveness—if you usually agree to everything, try saying no and enjoy the freedom of doing so. The potential to be assertive is there, and you may begin to feel more confident as a result of being assertive.

The calculation that needs to be done to find your birth date number is relatively simple:

First: Write out your full date of birth.

Example: 21 June 1967

Second: Write your date of birth in its numerical form.

Example: 21/06/1967

Step 1: Add together the numbers in each section of your birth date.

Example: $2 + 1 = 3$; $0 + 6 = 6$; $1 + 9 + 6 + 7 = 23$

Step 2: Add together the three totals.

Example: $3 + 6 + 23 = 32$

Step 3: Add these two numbers together to reduce the number to 1 in the range of 1 to 9 (using the process of fadic addition).

Example: $3 + 2 = 5$

Step 4: This should now be a number between 1 and 9 and will be the birth date number.

Example: Hence the person in our example has the birth date number 5.

Example 2: 14 September 1941

   14/09/1941

   Step 1: $1 + 4 = 5$; $0 + 9 = 9$; $1 + 9 + 4 + 1 = 15$

   Step 2: $5 + 9 + 15 = 29$

   Step 3: $2 + 9 = 11$; $1 + 1 = 2$

In this example it was necessary to do a further step at Step 3 as the one procedure did not reduce the number to one digit between 1 and 9.

Birth Date Number One

Positive Characteristics

People born with Birth Date Number One are decisive and independent. They make strong and effective leaders as they are assertive, confident and perceptive. Number One people often reach the top in their chosen careers because they are self-motivated and focused on success. They are often of higher than average intelligence and use this to their advantage. Birth Date Number One is strongly linked with creative talents and originality.

Negative Characteristics

People born with Birth Date Number One can tend to be self-centred and have narrow vision as a result of their self-confidence and determination to succeed. They can be rather tyrannical in their attempts to lead, and other people often find them domineering and dictatorial. Number Ones are not good at negotiating and can be stubborn and uncooperative. Number Ones can be their own worst enemies if they set themselves unachievable goals that cannot be met. This in turn can lead to frustration.

Relationships

Number Ones will often find that they have many relationships before they settle down. They have high expectations of their partners and will often be disappointed if they find that their mate does not meet these expectations. Number Ones should be aware that they may be seeking a perfect partner who does not exist.

It would be wise for Number Ones to assess what they really want from a relationship and with whom they are likely to achieve this. Number Ones should accept their own limitations as well as their partners in order for a relationship to succeed. To maintain a happy and healthy relationship, Number Ones will need to make a concerted effort to prioritize their relationships and allow time in their lives to spend with their partners.

People born with the Number One birth number often need a lot of reassurance and praise from their partners in order to boost their self-esteem. Number Ones should remember, however, that their partners will need this to be reciprocated.

Relationships will tend not to be the priority in the lives of Number Ones as they do not regard it as an area in which success can be measured. The focus of their lives will tend to be careers or material gain, and this can put relationships in the shadow. As a result, Number Ones are frequently loners and are often content to be so.

Parenthood
Number Ones are loving and dedicated parents who tend to be committed to the rearing of their children. Family is important to Number Ones, and they will want to have a strong bond with their children. As parents, Number Ones will wish to be involved in their children's lives and will encourage them to fulfil their potential. They should be wary not to dominate their children but allow them the opportunity to develop their own interests. Number One parents should not have overly high expectations for their children as they may not be able to hide their frustrations if they are disappointed. As

long as Number One parents allow their children plenty of growing space they should have a good relationship.

Home and Leisure
It is important for Number Ones to have a comfortable and warm home where they can relax. Number Ones should try to relax as much as possible when at home. They may find that by developing their creative talents they are able to un-wind. They may find that they enjoy writing, music, art, etc. It is unlikely that a Number One would not have creative talents that could be developed as most people with this birth date number are gifted in some way.

Number Ones enjoy a good time and can often live life to excess. They are often guilty of burning the candle at both ends, which may eventually take its toll. Number Ones should be aware of their excesses and try to balance them within their lives.

Career
Number Ones are suited to careers that make the most of their creative talents but also allow them the opportunity to excel and succeed. People born with Birth Date Number One should be aware that they do not work well as part of a team, because they are fiercely ambitious and need to dominate a group. They need time on their own and space to be creative in their work.

Number Ones will often find themselves drawn towards the performing arts as they will be the focus of attention and their success will be obvious to all. It is important to recognize that this is a highly competitive area of work and that not everyone can succeed in this field. However, Number Ones are more likely than most to find success in this environment.

Other careers that would suit Number Ones are those of designer, journalist, writer and engineer. Number Ones will often know the career that they are interested in following and will pursue their goals in this area.

Colour
Number Ones should include the colour yellow in their lives as it is a bold colour that represents success.

Famous Number Ones

Robert Redford	Sean Connery
Paul Gascoigne	Sophia Loren
Rolf Harris	Virginia Wolf
Angus Deayton	Mother Teresa

Birth Date Number Two

Positive Characteristics
People born with Birth Date Number Two are often skilled diplomats. They have the ability to compromise and negotiate. Number Twos are charming and considerate of others, which makes them popular. They tend to be peace-loving and are able to cooperate with others in order to maintain

harmony in their lives. Number Two people are often compassionate and caring, with a strong sense of right and wrong. They tend to be selfless as they are focused on the greater good of all.

Negative Characteristics

Number Twos will naturally shy away from conflict, and this can result in issues not being resolved. People born with Birth Date Number Two will often not fulfil their potential in their careers as they lack the motivation to pursue success even if they have the desire and the ability to succeed. Number Twos can lack confidence in themselves and their ideas, despite the respect of others. Self-doubt can often influence the actions of Number Twos, and they often do not act decisively. Number Twos should be wary of becoming pessimistic and cynical because this will hold them back unnecessarily.

Relationships

Number Twos are committed and faithful to their partners and will expect the same in return. People born with Birth Date Number Two will make every effort to ensure that their relationships are successful and will not be likely to make a break in any situation. For this reason, Number Twos should be wary of making a commitment to the wrong person and should consider a relationship seriously before settling down.

Number Twos enjoy socializing and are generally well

liked. They are often noted for their sense of humour. Number Twos will find that they have many admirers but should check their compatibility with a potential partner before coming involved. Number Twos need security in their lives and should look for a partner who will provide this.

Once in a relationship, Number Twos are adaptable and open to change as long as they feel happy and secure within the relationship. Mutual respect and appreciation are of utmost importance to Number Twos in relationships. Without this, insecurity will begin to cast a shadow over them. Number Twos will react very badly to infidelity or betrayal of trust, and they may become bitter and jealous.

Parenthood
Number Twos as parents will ensure that their children are raised in a warm and loving environment. Their children will feel secure and supported by their parents, who will allow them freedom to develop independently but will always be there if needed. As the home is so important to Number Twos, they will strive to create the most comfortable and secure home for their families.

Number Two parents should be honest with their children if there are domestic difficulties for they will feel inclined to try to cover up any difficulties to maintain the feeling of security and happiness. Children will be aware that they are being left out and may resent this.

Home and Leisure

The home is an important place for Number Twos, and they will spend a great deal of time making the most of it. Many Number Twos have leisure interests related to the home, such as DIY, sewing, flower arranging, gardening, etc. Number Twos find a sense of reward from spending time on an activity that has tangible results.

Number Twos enjoy socializing and will seldom find themselves short of invitations. People consider Number Twos to be good friends and will want to spend time with them.

Number Twos are health-conscious and have an interest in alternative lifestyles. Many Number Twos are vegetarians and have an interest in aromatherapy, acupuncture, reflexology, etc.

Career

The Number Two temperament is well suited to caring professions, and they will often find themselves employed as social workers, doctors, nurses, etc. Working for voluntary organizations will also appeal to Number Twos, who need to feel a sense of purpose in their work. Number Twos will settle well in careers where they feel that they are benefiting others.

Number Twos will not flourish in a competitive work environment as they will not respond well to wrangling and disputes. Number Twos who find themselves in such situations will become disillusioned and their motivation will evaporate.

Colour
Number Two people will appreciate the colour blue, which is a calm and soothing colour that reflects their personality.

Famous Number Twos

Princess Anne	Andrew Lloyd Webber
Gerry Adams	Madonna
Tony Blair	Cliff Richard
Henry Ford	Julie Andrews
Beatrix Potter	Noel Edmonds
Robert Louis Stevenson	Jane Fonda

Birth Date Number Three

Positive Characteristics
Number Threes are charming people with a childlike quality of innocence. They have a good sense of humour and a real interest in other people, which makes them very popular. Number Threes have a special talent for interacting with other people, and they enjoy talking to others and making them laugh. Number Threes are naturally optimistic and tend to enjoy life to the full. They are able to cope with life's ups and downs and will not be disheartened for long by any setbacks.

Negative Characteristics
A fondness for the limelight can be a fault found in Number

Threes. Others can resent the show-off side of the Number Three character and become resentful. Number Threes are likely to be oblivious to any resentment—they are frequently social butterflies and will move from one social gathering to another with ease but without really getting to know the other people. Naivety is another aspect of the Number Three character that can work against people born with this number. Number Threes can often be fooled by people who appear to be genuine friends but who really mean them harm. Number Threes should be wary of accepting people on face value and should try to see behind people's facades.

Relationships
Number Threes have high expectations of their partners. Their ideal partners are exceptionally attractive and are individuals who stand out from the crowd. Relationships to Number Threes are very romantic affairs filled with poetry and flowers. It is not surprising that a Number Three person is often disappointed once he or she settles down into a relationship and finds himself or herself discussing whose turn it is to do the dishes. Number Threes need excitement and romance and if faced with domestic drudgery may look elsewhere for excitement.

Number Threes are naturally flirtatious people and they will find that they have a great many admirers. Finding a partner will not be difficult for Number Threes, but they should choose people with similar interests if they are hoping for a long-term commitment. For a lasting relationship, Number Threes need to find someone who shares their fondness for socializing and romance.

Parenthood

Number Threes are fun-loving parents. They view their children as equals and will enjoy sharing new experiences together. Number Three parents will spend a lot of time talking to their children, discussing the exciting events of the day. As parents, Number Threes will encourage their children to be sociable and will put on extravagant parties for their children and their friends.

Number Three parents should not allow their children to take second place to their social lives, which can be a danger once the novelty of parenthood begins to wear off. Number Three parents should allow their children plenty of time and should be there to help their children through any difficult patches.

Home and Leisure

To Number Threes, the home should be a place that is welcoming to other people, a place where social events can happen. Number Threes will furnish their homes in a haphazard way, with different styles and designs in one room. They have a natural flair, though, and the result tends to be successful.

Number Threes live for socializing—they like nothing better than getting ready to go out to a good party. They are often well known in the local eating and drinking establishments, where they will be regular visitors. Number Threes will often be found to be involved in local activities, such as coffee mornings and jumble sales, where they can meet up with their neighbours. Number Threes will rarely spend time on their own and do not like solitary activities.

Number Threes enjoy team sports that allow them the opportunity to bond with their team-mates. Individual sports hold no interest for Number Threes.

Career

Number Threes will nearly always be found in careers that involve working with people. Their flair for communication often results in them finding employment as sales representatives, teachers or public relations officers. Number Threes often have a flair for the written word and are often successful writers.

Number Threes should avoid work that does not involve social interaction or that requires regular nine to five attendance. Number Threes will not hold down a routine office job for long—they will find little motivation for this type of work.

Number Threes will probably have a variety of careers. They will not be likely to hold down one job for more than a few years. They will find that once they have adapted to one job they will begin to look to the future and gaining some new skill or experience. They will want to broaden their horizons wherever possible. They are unlikely to reach the top of their careers because they frequently change them. This will not dishearten Number Threes, however. To them new experiences and variety are far more important than success and material wealth.

Colour
Purple is the colour favoured by Number Threes. It is a colour that reflects their personality well—subtly attractive and luxurious.

Famous Number Threes

David Bowie	Casanova
Queen Victoria	Robert Burns
Roald Dahl	Honor Blackman
Audrey Hepburn	Rod Stewart

Birth Date Number Four

Positive Characteristics
Number Fours are hard-working, loyal and ambitious. They have a great deal of common sense and a practical approach to life. Number Fours are careful and are unlikely to make a decision without giving the matter a great deal of thought. Once Number Fours have reached a decision they will be determined on their decided course of action. Other people depend on Number Fours' ability to cope with life's ups and downs. People are drawn to the stability of Number Fours. Number Fours are reliable friends and once they have de-

cided that they like someone they will not change their opinion easily.

Negative Characteristics

Number Fours are very traditional and find any challenges to the status quo difficult to accept. They find it hard to disguise their disapproval of flighty and superficial people or of people living alternative lifestyles. Number Fours have a distrust of the unknown and are far more comfortable with things within their ken. This can lead to intolerance of other people who choose to follow a different path. Number Fours should try to be more open to change and accept others for what they are.

Number Fours' ambitions can be a source of stress if they are found to be out of reach. When stressed, Number Fours become ill-tempered and often lash out at whoever is nearest at hand. Number Fours should learn to manage their stress in other ways in order to avoid unnecessary conflicts.

Relationships

Number Fours approach love and relationships seriously, and they are unlikely to play the field. Long-term commitment is likely to be the priority for Number Fours. Other people will be attracted by the stability and security offered by Number Fours, and in turn Number Fours will be attracted to vulnerable people who need more control in their lives.

Generally, Number Fours are loving, considerate and caring partners. They will be protective of their chosen partners and will be faithful and dependable.

Number Fours should be careful not to dominate their partners but should allow them plenty of freedom and space to be individuals. Number Fours find it difficult to express their emotions openly to their partners, and this may be interpreted as a lack of feeling. Partners of Number Fours should accept that their mates are not prone to romantic outpourings but that they demonstrate their affection in other ways. Number Fours should make attempts to be open with their partners.

Stress in the lives of Number Fours can create difficulties if they direct their frustrations at their partners. Number Fours will often take stress home and create arguments in order to cope with their personal difficulties. Number Fours and their partners should be aware that this is a trait that exists and work out a strategy for dealing with it. It is especially important that Number Fours are honest and open about their emotions in these situations or they may jeopardize their relationships.

Parenthood

Number Four parents care a great deal about their children and want the best for them. Family traditions are important to Number Fours, and they will want their children to be involved in activities. Difficulties may arise as their children become teenagers and want to explore the alternative options that life has to offer. Number Four parents want the best for their children and will believe that they know what is the right course of action. It is important that as parents they accept their children's right to make independent decisions whatever they may be.

Home and Leisure

Home is important to Number Fours. They can relax only in an organized and orderly environment and will go to great lengths to make their home suitable. Number Fours will get satisfaction from housework, gardening and other pursuits with visible benefits. Spending time organizing and tidying is very therapeutic for Number Fours and can be developed as a form of stress management.

Number Fours are unlikely to enjoy socializing to a large extent. They do not enjoy noisy gatherings where they come into contact with flighty and superficial people. Number Fours prefer more sedate social occasions and enjoy having a few close friends round for a meal or drinks.

Number Fours should develop more leisure activities that help to alleviate the stress from which they suffer. They may enjoy sports but should avoid competitive ones that may increase their stress levels. Mountain climbing or hillwalking may be suitable hobbies as Number Fours will enjoy the challenge and be able to see what they have accomplished.

Career

Number Fours are very career-minded and are highly ambitious in this area. In return for hard work and loyalty, Number

Fours will expect appreciation and recognition. If Number Fours feel that their efforts are not being acknowledged, they will become ill-tempered and frustrated. Number Fours are focused on success and will let nothing stand in the way of achieving it. They can be insensitive towards the feelings of others who may get in their way.

Number Fours will be happiest in a smaller firm where their loyalty and determination is more likely to be noticed and rewarded. If Number Fours feel that they are working together towards a common goal, they will be able to focus their determination towards the benefit of the company. As bosses, Number Fours are fair and reasonable leaders. Number Fours have the unusual gift of being able to learn from their mistakes and recognizing that they may have been in the wrong, which is invaluable as an employer.

Number Fours are often successful at setting up their own businesses. As their own bosses they are able to be clear about the focus of their efforts and will be able to measure the extent of their success.

Colour

Red is a beneficial colour for Number Fours. It is a colour that will enhance their confidence and reflect their determination to succeed.

Famous Number Fours

Queen Elizabeth II	Linford Christie
John Major	Cilla Black

Richard Branson   Clint Eastwood

Dolly Parton   Margaret Thatcher

Birth Date Number Five

Positive Characteristics

The most common trait found in Number Fives is their ability to adapt and change. Number Fives are free spirits who have a sense of adventure and a curiosity about life. They have a desire to expand their horizons and gain insights into the lifestyles of other cultures. Number Five people are easy going and happy-go-lucky. They are friendly and approachable, with a talent for finding common ground with nearly everyone they meet.

Negative Characteristics

The person born with Birth Date Number Five is always prepared to take a chance and may get into difficult situations as a result of an impulsive decision. Number Fives should try to balance their impulsive natures with common sense in order to avoid unnecessary risks. Unfortunately, not all the people whom Number Fives meet will share their open-minded approach to life, and they may encounter people who are offended by their lifestyle. Number Fives are unaware of the motivation of other people and may not realize that not everyone wishes them well.

Number Fives have a tendency to know a little about a great number of subjects but to be expert in none. Because they are always looking to the future, to what they can learn about next, they do not bother to research the current subject fully but learn enough to have a superficial understanding. This can be an irritating trait to people who regard themselves as experts and resent the attitude of Number Fives. Number Fives, however, are unlikely to be aware of the resentment.

Relationships

Number Fives are likely to have many relationships. They are adventurous in the area of romance and want to have a wide variety of experiences. Their easy-going natures and interest in people means that they will never be short of admirers. Number Fives find most people attractive and interesting and so will take up many of the offers.

Number Fives are naturally wary of commitment and responsibility, and will be reluctant to settle down. They will not give their partners false hope, however—they will not make promises that they do not intend to keep. The partner of a Number Five will know where he or she stands. If Number Fives declare their love for their partners then this will be an indication that they are serious and wish to make a commitment.

If Number Fives experience difficulties in their relationships they will be likely to avoid the problem and may look for solace elsewhere. However, Number Fives will find no pleasure from infidelities as the problem that they were trying to run away from will still exist and they will have introduced a new difficulty. Number Fives should be aware that discussing and recognizing difficulties can strengthen a relationship and avoid future difficulties.

Number Fives are loving and caring, and partners can be sure that life will never be dull with a Number Five in their lives. Once a common understanding has been achieved, relationships between Number Fives and their partners will generally be harmonious.

Parenthood
Number Fives are committed to being good parents and will give their children all the support and encouragement that they need. As parents, Number Fives are aware of the importance of allowing their children space and respect to choose their own direction. Number Fives and their children will generally enjoy relationships based on mutual respect.

Home and Leisure
Number Fives have a wide diversity of interests and will spend their leisure time expanding their knowledge and experiences. They are keen to learn about alternative lifestyles and have an interest in politics but lack the commitment to become involved in either. They spend a great deal of time dipping into books, watching films, documentaries, etc, and discussing what they have learned with friends.

Number Fives will accept invitations to gatherings where they will be able to get into discussions with other people.

Their love of conversation means that they will not want to go to noisy nightclubs.

Travel is a common interest for Number Fives, and they will frequently plan their next adventures on their way home from their most recent journeys. Travel for Number Fives should be an opportunity to expand their knowledge of other cultures, and package holidays to Spain, etc, will leave them cold. More exotic destinations are likely to appeal to Number Fives or, if finances do not allow this, they will want to go somewhere away from the usual tourist resorts closer to home.

Home could be anywhere to Number Fives, and they are able to put down roots and feel comfortable wherever they find themselves. Number Fives will not spend their time creating the perfect home because they could easily pack up and move on at a moment's notice.

Career

Careers are not important to Number Fives. Work is merely a means to an end, to fund their lifestyle and allow them the money to travel. Number Fives do not like responsibility and will not feel a sense of commitment to their employers. They need freedom in their lives and find the routine structure of work a bind. Number Fives are disinclined to tackle any difficulties in their workplace. If they are unhappy they will simply move on.

Number Fives do best when they have careers that incorporate their interests and talents. Careers in the travel business have an obvious attraction, and Number Fives flourish as travel agents and holiday reps. Occupations that allow Number Fives to make the most of their communication skills are equally suitable, and they can become accomplished teachers and lecturers.

People born with Birth Date Number Five will probably change careers many times, especially in their twenties and thirties. Later in life Number Fives are more likely to feel able to settle down to one career once they have explored many of their interests.

Colour
Orange is a colour that is well suited to people born with Birth Date Number Five. It reflects their bright cheerful and positive nature.

Famous Number Fives

Mary Queen of Scots	Terry Wogan
Charlotte Brontë	Doris Day
John Cleese	Vincent Van Gogh
Tina Turner	James Joyce
Dudley Moore	

Birth Date Number Six

Positive Characteristics
People born with Birth Date Number Six are very fortunate as it reflects harmony and balance. Number Six people are

stylish and have the ability to command the attention of others. Number Sixes have charisma, and people are often drawn to them. They are trusted by others and often find themselves involved in other people's problems because of their impartiality, their ability to listen and to see the potential for compromise. People recognize that Number Sixes are non-judgmental and tolerant of other people's differences, and so they often want to talk through their problems with Number Sixes. Number Sixes are trustworthy characters and would be unlikely to take advantage of their position as confidant.

Negative Characteristics
Number Sixes are undoubtedly talented in dealing with the problems of other people but unfortunately are unable to deal with their own difficulties. There is a tendency in Number Sixes to put on a brave face and to hide any emotional turmoil. The result of this is that anxieties are not dealt with and are internalized. This trait does not only make the lives of Number Sixes stressful but can also make them appear to be inhuman to those who know them. People can become resentful of the fact that nothing ever seems to go wrong for Number Sixes, and they can be regarded as smug and self-satisfied.

Number Sixes should be more honest with themselves and others about their feelings and should find ways to cope with difficulties. Internalizing stress will take its toll in the future, and it is better to deal with it in the present.

Relationships

Number Sixes are often extremely attractive individuals with a great deal of sex appeal. Although many people may flirt with Number Sixes and be flattered by their attentions, they may not regard Number Sixes as the type they wish to settle down with. Number Sixes can be seen as too attractive to be trusted.

Number Sixes can find it difficult to find a suitable partner. They are often drawn to people who project the right image, however, and this can lead to disappointment for Number Sixes if they have fallen for the image rather than the person. It may be wiser for Number Sixes to look for a partner who will meet their emotional needs, someone sensitive and understanding. If Number Sixes find such a mate, they may be able to begin to deal with their stresses and emotional difficulties. In relationships, Number Sixes need lots of affection and reassurance, and their partners should be aware that they may be hiding negative emotions.

Number Sixes demonstrate their affection through making a fuss of their partners on significant dates such as birthdays and anniversaries. They are not comfortable in demonstrating affection on a daily basis as they have a deep-rooted fear of rejection.

Arguments are unlikely in a relationship with a Number Six as the people born with this birth date number are likely to compromise and negotiate in order to avoid a dispute. Number Sixes should be honest if they harbour resentment or ill-feelings and should allow their partners to do the same—discussing these will minimize future disagreements on the same topic.

Parenthood

The family unit is of utmost importance to Number Sixes, and they make proud parents. They will take great pride in their children's achievements and will always prioritize events such as school concerts. They should be wary of pressurizing their children to succeed and should not place too much emphasis on academic achievements. Number Six parents should be prepared to accept that their children will not necessarily choose to follow a conventional path in their lives and should not try to prevent their children making their own choices.

Home and Leisure

Number Sixes will furnish their homes with high quality goods. They are not concerned with flashy or expensive items but do like to invest their money wisely. Their homes will tend to be tastefully decorated and to display comfort and security. Number Sixes, although not creatively talented, have an appreciation of fine arts and beautiful objects, which they will incorporate into their homes.

Number Sixes like to listen to classical music and opera, which can be an excellent form of relaxation. They also enjoy reading good quality fiction. The social events that appeal to Number Sixes tend to be low-key, for example, they enjoy the company and conversation of a few good friends at a dinner or drinks party. Number Sixes enjoy board and card games, and may often be keen on games such as bridge, which combine their interests with socializing.

Career

Careers are not priorities in the lives of Number Sixes. Number Sixes are not competitive souls and find the cut and thrust of business unappealing; they do not like to be exposed to people's negative characteristics. The careers where Number Sixes flourish combine their talents and interests. Number Sixes are well suited to pursuing careers involving the arts, dealing, promoting, etc. Their negotiating abilities can lead to a career as a diplomat or personnel officer. Their style, flair and artistic eye can be developed into a career as a make-up artist, fashion consultant or beautician.

Colour

Green is the colour that favours people born with Birth Date Number Six as it is a well-balanced colour that reflects harmony and contentment.

Famous Number Sixes

Prince Edward   Laura Ashley

Tony Benn   Agatha Christie

John McEnroe	Michael Caine
D H Lawrence	Greta Garbo
Oswald Mosely	Glenda Jackson
Thomas Edison	Michael Jackson

Birth Date Number Seven

Positive Characteristics

People born with Birth Date Number Seven are sensitive and compassionate. They have a natural wisdom and ability to see to the truth of matters. Once people get to know a Number Seven, they will find an exceptional person who is able to offer warmth, sympathy and understanding. Number Sevens take their time to consider problems and weigh up the pros and cons of any given situation before coming to their conclusion. Number Seven people are adaptable and adjust easily to change. This tends to be because they are generally happy within themselves.

Negative Characteristics

Number Sevens often lack confidence in their abilities. They do not like to draw attention to themselves, and as a result their talents often go unnoticed. As a result of their lack of confidence, many Number Sevens find it difficult to communicate effectively with other people and can come across as being vague. There is a tendency for Number Sevens to be dreamers as they spend so much of their time immersed in their own thoughts. They should be wary of becoming cut off from the outside world and should make the effort to socialize with their friends.

Relationships

Number Seven people are extremely romantic and fall head over heals in love easily. They have a tendency to declare their undying love in the very early stages of a relationship, and this can be off-putting for the object of their affections, who may feel that things are moving too fast. Number Sevens should try to keep their emotions in check more and to let relationships grow at a more sedate pace. This approach is more likely to allow Number Sevens to discover if what they are experiencing is love or is in fact a brief infatuation.

Number Sevens are demonstrative in their affection and frequently express their love and devotion to their partners. The people who are most likely to be attracted to Number Seven people are those who find it difficult to express their emotions and feel that their inability can be compensated for by the more than plentiful abilities of Number Sevens. This generally is a good balance but can lead to problems. Number Sevens will need to be reassured and have their declarations reciprocated from time to time or they will become insecure and begin to doubt their partners' love. In this situation Number Sevens should be honest about how they are feeling and let their partners know that they need to be appreciated. Number Sevens often choose partners who are less dreamy than themselves and are more gifted in practical matters, and again this is a good balance.

Parenthood

Number Sevens approach the duties of parenthood very seriously. They are committed parents, and the necessity for commitment can make them take a more realistic approach to life. As parents, Number Seven people will do whatever is necessary to provide their children with what they need but do this without overindulging or spoiling their children. Number Seven parents have very strong affection for their children, and they will be likely to have a close relationship with them throughout their lives. The children of Number Seven parents will appreciate the love and devotion that they receive and will usually choose to spend a great deal of time at the family home.

Home and Leisure

Number Sevens enjoy outdoor pursuits such as mountain climbing. They love to see dramatic landscapes and enjoy the freedom from the harsh realities of their everyday lives. Sport in general has an attraction for Number Sevens—they enjoy escaping into the tactics and strategies required by many sports.

Number Sevens are also frequently enthusiastic readers, enjoying all types of literature. Number Sevens find books that give an insight into human nature to be particularly appealing, and they will often be found reading nonfiction, history, and autobiographies.

The homes of Number Sevens will reflect their desire for harmony and peace. The furnishings and decor will tend to be soothing and calming but not luxurious or extravagant. Number Sevens will spend a lot of time relaxing in their homes, and it is an important place for them.

Socializing is not a regular pastime of Number Sevens. They can find the effort to communicate quite stressful and may not find it easy to relax in large groups. Smaller social occasions with close friends are more likely to appeal, but even these will not be regular events.

Career

Number Sevens are not driven by ambition and have no desire for excessive material wealth. They are hard-working and committed individuals, but they must feel that their hard work benefits the world at large, not just themselves. For this reason, Number Sevens are often found working in voluntary organizations and the caring professions. For some Number Sevens, their desire for escapism could be met by a career in the travel industry—the opportunity to visit far-off places combined with ensuring that others enjoy their holiday can be a very rewarding combination.

Honesty and independence are admirable qualities found in Number Sevens, but these can cause difficulties in some working environments. Number Sevens will never let a dishonest act or an act that offends their sense of integrity go unchallenged. This can lead to Number Sevens challenging their employers and creating an unwanted scene. It is important for Number Sevens to accept that there are some professions that require a certain amount of flexibility and that they may not be suited to careers in such areas of work. If they do choose a career in one of these professions, Number Sevens will need to refrain from challenging their employers if they wish to succeed.

Colour
Grey is a colour that Number Sevens will feel comfortable with. It is a calm and soothing colour that reflects the desire of Number Sevens to blend in. Bold colours should be avoided by Number Sevens.

Famous Number Sevens

Jilly Cooper	Bob Geldof
Saddem Hussein	Muhammad Ali
Kingsley Amis	Eric Clapton
Anthony Trollope	Winston Churchill
Mel Gibson	Freddie Mercury
Marilyn Monroe	Diana, Princess of Wales
Emma Thompson	

Birth Date Number Eight

Positive Characteristics
People born with Birth Date Number Eight are generally content and sure of themselves. Such confidence is found in Number Eights because they know themselves well and are aware of their strengths and abilities. Focused and practical, Number Eights know what they want from life and know how they are going to achieve their goals. Number Eights rarely set themselves unachievable targets. They are realists and assess their capabilities and opportunities before deciding on their ambitions.

Number Eights are dependable characters and would never let anyone down. Responsibility is taken very seriously by Number Eights, and they can always be relied upon by others. Determined and strong-willed, Number Eights will never betray their own beliefs or another's trust.

Negative Characteristics
The determination of Number Eights can be overzealous at times, and they can become stubborn and unbending in their pursuit of their goals. Number Eights are so sure of themselves that they do not ever consider the possibility of being in the wrong. They will not compromise or negotiate because they are certain that they know best. This aspect of their character can be very damaging, and it can appear that Number

Eights have no concern for other people's thoughts and feelings. This is not the case but an understandable conclusion that can be drawn from their actions.

Number Eights should learn to listen to other people more and to hear what they are being told. It is very important for them to realize that everyone is fallible and prone to making mistakes and that Number Eights are no exception to the rule. If Number Eights learn to negotiate and compromise, they may find that they can actually learn from other people and improve their chances of achieving their goals.

Relationships

Number Eights have a fear of expressing their emotions. They are frightened of rejection and being hurt. Anyone involved with a Number Eight will need to initiate any discussions about love or commitment as Number Eights will never expose themselves emotionally if they are unsure of the response they will receive.

Early in life Number Eights will not be overly concerned with romance or relationships—they are more likely to focus their attentions on their ambitions in other areas of their lives. Later in life, however, finding a partner and making a commitment may become an ambition in itself. Relationships formed by Number Eights later in life are more likely to succeed as they will have more energy and attention to devote to their partners once their other ambitions are realized.

If Number Eights do form relationships in their youth, they

should try to set aside time to spend with their partners and remember to include their partners in their plans for the future.

Parenthood

As parents, Number Eights will want to ensure that their children are raised in an environment that is secure and comfortable. They will want their children to have the best of everything and will spare no expense in providing for them. Number Eights find parenthood less stressful later in life when they are more likely to have the financial means to provide for their children. They will also have more time to spend with their children, which they will find very rewarding. The children of Number Eight parents will know that they can always turn to their parents for support and security.

Home and Leisure

Sports that have an element of a challenge will appeal to Number Eights. They like the excitement and sense of achievement of overcoming the odds, and will often be attracted to sports such as rock climbing and potholing.

Any activity that has an obvious finished result will make Number Eights happy. Pleasure could be derived from the simple act of completing a difficult jigsaw puzzle.

The homes of Number Eights will reflect their confidence and contentment. Number Eights will enjoy putting their practical skills to use about the home and will take pleasure in DIY. Number Eights have a passion for gadgets, and their homes will be full of labour-saving devices. Unlike many people, Number Eights will make full use of their appliances.

Career

Number Eights have strong ambitions and a deep desire to succeed. They are prepared to work hard and commit themselves totally to their careers in the pursuit of success. Work can in fact become something of an obsession for Number Eights, and they should try to achieve a better balance between work and pleasure.

Efficient workers who know how to use their initiative, Number Eights are valuable employees and have a great deal to offer an employer. The organizational skills, motivation and enthusiasm of Number Eights are respected and valued by employers, and Number Eights' hard work usually results in swift promotion.

As managers, Number Eights are skilled and fair. Decision making does not daunt Number Eights, and they are happy to make important decisions and to carry the responsibility for the consequences. Number Eights recognize the importance of team work and working together towards a common goal. They will encourage members of their team to make the most of their personal abilities and skills. It is important for Number Eights to share power and responsibility in the workplace and not take on all the pressure alone.

Number Eights are well suited to careers in finance and

marketing but also do well in setting up their own businesses.

Colour
Muted reds, greens and purples will appeal to Number Eights—they are comfortable and confident colours that also have an element of luxuriousness. If feeling stressed, Number Eights should experiment with lighter colours.

Famous Number Eights

John F Kennedy	George Orwell
Pope John Paul II	Joan Collins
Elizabeth Taylor	Rex Harrison
Frank Bruno	Oscar Wilde
Liza Minnelli	Jeffrey Archer

Birth Date Number Nine

Positive Characteristics
People born with Birth Date Number Nine are independent, courageous and resilient. Optimists by nature, Number Nines have a happy-go-lucky approach to life, and they are more than able to cope with life's ups and downs. Number Nines are sure of themselves and are generally content with their lot.

Once set on a course of action, Number Nines will follow their chosen course with determination—they will not be put off or disheartened. Their enthusiasm and vitality can have a positive impact on other people who tend to get carried along with Number Nines' energy. Number Nines have hidden depths—they have a great deal of sympathy and understanding for their fellow human beings. They are non-judgmental of others and are happy to accept people for what they are.

Negative Characteristics

A forceful and uncompromising approach to life will get many Number Nines where they want to be but can cause other people great distress. Number Nines do not enjoy conflict or hurting others, and so this aspect of their character needs to be kept in check. It is important for Number Nines to recognize that, unlike themselves, not everyone finds it easy to bounce back from disappointments and that other people may hurt for a long time after they have moved on. Quick tempers are common amongst Number Nines, as is a tendency to lash out at whoever is nearest to hand.

Number Nines are often guilty of being self-centred and of not listening to others. They have such a belief in themselves that they are not willing to listen to the opinions of others, which can cause resentment.

Relationships

Number Nines are an attractive lot. If they lack traditional charms, they will certainly compensate with more than a fair measure of sex appeal. Never short of admirers, Number Nines tend to enjoy a hectic love life.

Number Nines are in love with the idea of being in love—

they adore romantic gestures and are easily won over by candlelit dinners and poetry. Once Number Nines fall in love, they will do so wholeheartedly and will swear their undying love and devotion—this will not necessarily be reciprocated by the object of their desire. If they receive a cautious response, they will decide that the relationship is not for them and look elsewhere. Number Nines thrive on passion and excitement, and a relationship lacking these qualities is unlikely to satisfy them.

Relationships are very important to Number Nines, and they will be loving and affectionate partners. They will ensure that romance and passion are kept alive in their relationships. However, their emotional and passionate natures can cause problems. They are very susceptible to jealousy and are likely to create scenes and throw tantrums if they feel they have grounds for suspicion or are faced with the behaviour of a flirtatious partner.

Parenthood
Number Nines will generally have good relationships with their children. Arguments may be commonplace, but they will not be of a serious nature. The only real problem that may arise is if Number Nines become jealous of the attention that their children receive. In this situation Number Nines should be honest about their jealousy and try to arrange time alone with their partners so that they can fully enjoy the times spent as a family.

Home and Leisure

Number Nines will have a busy and hectic social life and will never be short of invitations to social gatherings. Small gatherings of close friends are the ideal social occasions for Number Nines.

Number Nines have a liking for life's luxuries and are often found dining out at extravagant restaurants. At home, a bottle of fine wine will usually accompany every meal, and the larder and drinks cabinet will be well stocked with luxury items.

An appreciation of the finer things in life will be reflected throughout the homes of Number Nines. If finances permit, Number Nines will have a jacuzzi to bathe in and the best quality bed to sleep on. Number Nines will have the best of everything that they can afford, from top of the range music systems to electric toothbrushes.

Career

High pressure jobs appeal to Number Nines. They enjoy having to think on their feet and meet tight deadlines. Pressure motivates Number Nines, and in the right environment they can excel. They have great vision and are prepared to take bold steps that more cautious souls would shy away from.

In careers Number Nines like variety and will often change jobs on a regular basis in search of new and bigger challenges. Number Nines need work that constantly presents new challenges in order to maintain their enthusiasm and commitment. Once established in a career that suits their personalities, Number Nines have the potential to rise to the very top.

Number Nines are suited to careers in journalism, the armed forces, the police, the medical professions and finance—taking chances on the stock market will have a definite appeal to many Number Nines.

In dealing with colleagues, Number Nines should try to limit their criticisms and be patient with people who do not work at the frantic pace that they opt for. Number Nines will give credit where it is due and will be the first to applaud another colleague's hard work and input.

Colour
Brown is a colour favoured by Number Nines. It is a luxuriant colour that reflects confidence and security. It is also a soothing colour that can take the edge off the pressured lives of Number Nines.

Famous Number Nines

Nelson Mandela	Michael Palin
Dustin Hoffman	Barbara Cartland
Elvis Presley	Carl Jung
Bette Davis	Edna O'Brien
Harrison Ford	Anthony Hopkins

Compatibility

This chapter looks at the nine personality types dictated by birth date numbers and how they interact. The compatibility of each personality is detailed in the two key areas of Work and Romance.

Birth Date Personality Number One and Birth Date Personality Number One

Work
The combination of two Number Ones could be very powerful as both individuals are generally focused on success and have the ability to achieve the goals that they set themselves. They are creative and intelligent workers. If they recognize the talents in each other and decide to work together, they could form an invincible team.

The difficulty for these two individuals is in the setting of the ground rules for their professional relationship. Initially there could be a tendency for them to become rivals and to fight each other for dominance. Neither individual is likely to be willing to be told what to do, and neither is used to working in tandem with another individual. The focus of attention may become that of establishing superiority rather than succeeding in the world of business. The resulting impact would be a decline in both individuals' work performance.

For this working partnership to be successful, two Number Ones need to acknowledge their rivalry and to work together towards their common goal rather than using their creative powers to outdo each other. Two Number Ones each need to be allowed space and independence in the working environment and should recognize this need and accommodate it. Once they have established their respective roles, the two Number Ones will probably find that they enjoy working together and will gain a great deal from the experience. They will respect each other and probably become good friends.

Romance

For two Number Ones romantically involved with each other, it is important that they ensure that there is a balance of power in the relationship. It is important that one does not feel dominated by the other. The combination of two Number Ones together in romance can be extremely successful as there will be mutual respect and admiration. Another Number One is one of the few people likely to approach a Number One's idea of the perfect partner.

Problems could arise in this relationship because of the strong-willed nature of Number Ones. In an argument between two Number Ones, neither individual is likely to back down. Both are likely to be behaving in a selfish and stubborn way, but neither will be prepared to admit it. This is a problem that is likely to present itself time and time again in a relationship between two Number Ones. Neither individual will probably be overly concerned by this, and they will both just accept it as part of life.

Two Number Ones involved romantically should ensure that they set aside time from their hectic work and social lives for their relationship and spend time together. As these two share interests and ambitions it is a partnership that could endure the test of time.

Birth Date Personality Number One and Birth Date Personality Number Two

Work

The combination of Number One and Number Two is likely to form a good working partnership. The skills and talents of a Number One and Two will complement each other well. The ambition and drive of Number One will be balanced and kept in check by the diplomacy and tact of Number Two. Number One will provide the vision and creative spirit and Number Two will be the mediator in dealings with other people. Number One has the ability to make decisions and is happy to take on responsibility, which are areas that Number Two is less confident in. Number Two's talents lie in his or her ability to see the possibility for compromise and to persuade others to agree. Between them, Number One and Number Two have all the talents necessary for success.

Number One is a domineering character and may try to take advantage of Number Two by exploiting his or her gentle nature. Number Two will be offended if he or she feels that Number One is acting unfairly and will hold on to the resentment for a long time. Number One should be careful not to cross Number Two, who is more than capable of trying to right the wrong at a later date. If Number One tries to initiate arguments with Number Two, he or she will find that they have chosen the wrong person and will get no joy. Number One is not likely to persist in arguing with Number Two and will look for someone else to spar with.

As long as the balance in power does not tip too far in Number One's favour, this should be a successful working relationship. Both individuals will probably find the experience of working together a positive one and one from which they gain new skills.

Romance
In terms of romance, Number One and Number Two are quite well matched. Number Two will be able to meet the emotional needs of Number One and will be happy to supply the necessary reassurance and affection. The Number One in this relationship, however, should remember to reciprocate the warmth and affection and not take Number Two for granted. Number Two will understand that Number One needs space

and freedom and will do everything to ensure that this is provided.

Number One and Number Two will generally be happy together and are unlikely to have many arguments. Number One will probably snap at Number Two from time to time, but it is not in Number Two's nature to respond or create a scene. Number One will appreciate the quiet love and support provided by Number Two and will usually try not to be too irritable.

Number Two will stand by his or her Number One partner through thick and thin but should try to be assertive about his or her own needs rather than always providing for the loved one. It is important for Number Two to avoid becoming a doormat to Number One, not only to maintain his or her own self-esteem but to retain the respect of the partner.

Birth Date Personality Number One and Birth Date Personality Number Three

Work
Number One and Number Three are unlikely to encounter each other in the working environment as they do not share the same ambitions and goals. Number Three will want to work as part of a team and will be happy to do just enough to get by, whereas Number One will want to be the boss and to excel. The most likely scenario is for Number

Three to be working in a team with Number One in a managerial position.

If Number One and Number Three do find themselves working together, there is a possibility that they will complement each other, with Number One's ambitions being tempered by Number Three's contentment. Number Three may be able to provide the voice of reason in assessing the feasibility of Number One's ideas. Number One does not receive criticism well, however, and may dismiss Number Three's suggestions.

Number Three may see Number One as a bit of a tyrant and try to keep out of his or her way. Number Three will not be able to comprehend Number One's desire for success and will not be able to provide Number One with the encouragement and support that he or she needs. Number One is likely to view Number Three as lazy and unmotivated and will become irritated by his or her laidback approach. Number One may try to initiate arguments with Number Three but will soon discover that this has little positive impact on his or her work.

This is not likely to be a successful working relationship. It is also not likely to be long-lived. Number Three will soon change careers, especially if he or she feels that Number One is not providing support.

Romance
Number Three is likely to be attracted by the confidence and

ambition of Number One. A romance is a strong possibility between these two as Number One will be flattered by the attentions and admiration of Number Three.

Once a relationship is established, Number Three is not likely to impressed by the lack of attention from Number One. If Number One is seriously interested in Number Three and wants the relationship to work, he or she will have to learn to be more demonstrative and romantic. If Number Three feels unappreciated, there is a danger that he or she will look for romance with someone else. Number Three should accept that work and achieving goals is extremely important to Number One and that romance will not always be top of the agenda.

This combination will be most likely to succeed if the two individuals spend time getting to know each other and learning to understand each other's needs. It is important that throughout the relationship Number One and Number Three remember the other's needs and try and be supportive of each other.

Birth Date Personality Number One and Birth Date Personality Number Four

Work
The combination of Number One and Number Four can be the basis of an excellent working relationship. This working relationship will succeed only if Number One and

Number Four get to know each other and establish their respective roles so that they avoid competing with each other. If Number One and Number Four decide to work together, their combined ambitions and talents can lead to great success. Number Four's tolerance can be a good balance for Number One's single-mindedness.

Number One should be careful not accept all praise and recognition without acknowledging Number Four's hard work and considerable efforts. Number Four will become unhappy and resentful if he or she feels that Number One is taking all the credit for their joint work. Number One needs to give Number Four encouragement and praise. Time will iron out any difficulties that Number One and Number Four have in working with each other. It is important for each of them to recognize the other's needs and to make allowances accordingly. In the workplace Number Four should allow Number One space to be creative and Number One should ensure that Number Four has the opportunity to do practical work.

If Number One and Four can recognize and make the most of each other's skills and talents, they will find that they may have found the key to success. The experience of working together could be most rewarding for both individuals.

Romance
For this pairing to succeed, both individuals will need to be

committed to each other and to making the relationship work. The main problem facing this partnership is that both individuals wish to be dominant and to control the other. Neither party can accept another person trying to dictate to him or her, and this could be the source of much disharmony. Number Four's temper could give Number One reason to doubt the suitability of the match and may lead to a permanent rift. Number Four should learn to manage anger in a way that does not create conflict in the relationship.

By nature both Number One and Number Four are reluctant to be open about their emotions and so the relationship between the two may seem to lack open affection. Number One and Number Four should try to trust their partner and to be honest about how they are feeling. This is a relationship that needs to be worked at to succeed, but if the effort is put in then it could be rewarding for both parties.

Birth Date Personality Number One and Birth Date Personality Number Five

Work

Number One and Number Five are unlikely to work together—they have nothing in common when it comes to careers. It is unlikely that Number One and Number Five will choose to follow the same career, and if they do find themselves working at the same profession it will almost certainly be at different levels. Number Five has no ambition and is likely to be working in order to make ends meet. Number One, on the other hand, enjoys working and will be working towards career success.

Should Number One and Number Five end up working together, there will be a basic difficulty for them in understanding each other. Number One will find Number Five's lack of commitment and ambition hard to comprehend, and Number Five will in no way understand Number One's desire to succeed at his or her career. Number Five does not hold success in any form in much regard and may look at Number One with pity. Number One in turn may spare time to feel sorry for an underachiever like Number Five. Generally, Number One and Number Five will give each other little thought. It is unlikely that these two will have difficulties in working together because they are more likely simply to avoid each other in the workplace.

Romance
The main area of difficulty for this combination is initial attraction. There is little about Number One that Number Five will find attractive. Number Five will tend to regard Number One as a bit of a cold fish. Number One is unlikely to find Number Five's approach to life acceptable. Number Five is too irresponsible for Number One.

If this pair does get together, however, and they decide to commit to each other, the relationship has a fair chance of being successful. If Number Five does fall for Number One, he or she will have accepted Number One for what he or she is and will need to accept that they will have their differences. A relationship with Number Five may bring out another side to Number One's character. He or she may become more relaxed and carefree with Number Five as a partner. Number Five will be affectionate and supportive of Number One, and Number One will appreciate this attention. Number One should remember to pay attention to his or her partner too. There is a danger that Number Five will look elsewhere for affection if he or she feels that Number One is being neglectful. Number One should always make time to spend with his or her partner and not become too obsessed with work.

Once the few minor problems have been sorted out, Number One and Number Five will lead a happy life together. As long as Number One continues to put in effort, this should be a lasting union.

Birth Date Personality Number One and Birth Date Personality Number Six

Work

In order for this working relationship to be successful, Number One and Number Six need to get to know each other and to learn about each other's skills and ambitions. Number Six will tend to be wary of Number One's driving ambition and may feel threatened and intimidated. To perform well in a working environment, Number Six needs to be treated tactfully and respectfully. Number One may recognize the potential and creative skills of Number Six and wish to utilize them. The secret to success for this partnership really lies with Number One. The obstacles that are likely to exist will be in place because of Number One's tendency to be harsh and brusque with people. Number Six does not respond well to being ordered about. In order to make the most of working with Number Six, Number One will need to be less forceful and domineering in his or her approach. Once Number One realizes this and starts to be more pleasant to Number Six, there will be a noticeable improvement in the quality of work that they produce.

If a good working relationship is achieved then this is a partnership that could benefit both. Number One will learn to be less domineering and Number Six may realize that he or she occasionally needs to be more assertive.

Romance
Number Six's ability to project the right image will appeal to Number One, who may feel that he or she has found the ideal partner. If Number Six lives up to the expectations of Number One then the relationship may take off.

Difficulties may arise when it comes to displaying affection and emotions, as Number One is not naturally demonstrative and Number Six will not be open until he or she feels sure of the commitment of his or her partner.

This could result in the relationship petering out because neither party is sure how the other feels. Both Number One and Number Six should try to express how they feel about each other if they want the relationship to last. Number One needs to focus more attention on his or her relationship and to make more effort to be affectionate. Number Six should be assertive and occasionally take the lead in the relationship and express emotions and needs to his or her partner.

Honesty and openness form the basis of success for this couple. Number Six and Number One need to set aside time to spend with each other on a regular basis so that they can discuss the relationship and how they are feeling within it.

Birth Date Number Personality One and Birth Date Personality Number Seven

Work

The combination of Number One and Number Seven in the workplace is generally quite a successful one. Number Seven is not driven by the same ambition and need to dominate as Number One so there should not be any problems in establishing that Number One is the boss. Both individuals will be quite happy for Number One to take on the lion's share of responsibility and decision making. Number One will respect and admire the hard work that

Number Seven is willing to put in and will make sure that it is rewarded.

Problems may occur if Number Seven is given reason to suspect the integrity of Number One's work practices. Number One may feel that it is justifiable to bend the rules occasionally if the end result is success. Although he or she is capable of making a reasonable compromise, any dishonesty will deeply offend Number Seven, and he or she may well feel the need to make these misgivings public and would certainly challenge Number One. If this situation were to arise, it would be unlikely that either party would be willing to back down and compromise. Number One would not allow anything to stand in the way of success and Number Seven would under no circumstances accept a compromise if it involved dishonesty. This sort of scenario would almost certainly see the end of any working relationship between Number One and Number Seven.

This working partnership can only work if Number Seven feels that the work he or she is doing does not involve any dishonesty. Number One should be aware that to Number Seven integrity is of utmost importance.

Romance
This is an unlikely match as Number One and Number Seven have quite different interests and ideals. If, however, Number One and Number Seven do find themselves

attracted to each other and decide to become involved there is a fair chance that the relationship will work well. Number One and Number Seven will find each other interesting, and each will want to learn about how the other views different situations. This could lead to an interesting process of development for Number One and Number Seven, who will like having the opportunity to view the world through another's eyes.

Number Seven is very romantic and loving towards his or her partner. Number One will be happy to receive the support and affection of Number Seven but should also try to meet the needs of his or her partner, who also needs to be loved and supported. Number One should be careful not to neglect Number Seven or he or she may not tolerate the lack of affection and seek romance elsewhere. Difficulties may arise in this relationship if Number One tries to dominate Number Seven. Number Seven is very independent and will react badly to a domineering partner.

The key to success for this couple is communication and respect. Number One needs to make sure that he or she spends plenty of time with his or her Number Seven partner, and when they are together they should talk openly and honestly. Number One and Number Seven need to acknowledge and respect each other's individual needs.

Birth Date Personality Number One and Birth Date Personality Number Eight

Work

The combination of Number One and Number Eight in a working relationship has the potential to be exceptionally successful. Number One and Number Eight share a desire for success and both are driven by ambition. Neither is afraid to put in the hard work that is necessary in order to achieve goals. Both are talented and able individuals who have the capacity to realize their ambitions.

In order to form a successful working relationship, Number One and Number Eight need to work together as a team and not in opposition to each other. Problems will arise if Number One tries to dominate Number Eight, who is aware that he or she is more than Number One's equal. Number Eight will also become resentful if he or she feels that his or her hard work is not being properly recognized. Number One should try not to hog the limelight but let Number Eight receive due credit. Number Eight has a tendency to try to do everything alone and should try not to take on all the work but should acknowledge Number One's skills and talents and share the workload with him or her.

Once Number One and Number Eight get to know each other and reach an understanding, they will form a winning team. Together Number One and Number Eight could well achieve their ambitions in record time.

Romance

Number One and Number Eight have a great deal in common. They are both highly motivated and ambitious individuals who wish to succeed in their chosen careers. It is likely that there will be an instant attraction between these two, which will develop into admiration and respect from which romance could well blossom.

The combination of Number One and Number Eight in a relationship can be extremely beneficial to both individuals as they will be able to talk freely about their ambitions and goals with each other. Number One and Number Eight will both appreciate the opportunity to bounce ideas off each other and to discuss career issues. Both will feel supported and appreciated in this relationship, and they are likely to be very happy together

Number One and Number Eight share the tendency to neglect their romantic partners in favour of careers. This will not cause problems in this relationship as both individuals will appreciate each other's need to spend time on furthering their careers. It is important, however, that Number Eight and Number One do allow themselves time to spend together, and they should not let their relationship always take second place to their careers.

This relationship will not be very romantic or passionate but will probably stand the test of time admirably. Number One and Number Eight will both feel secure and content in their relationship with each other.

Birth Date Personality Number One and Birth Date Personality Number Nine

Work

The combination of Number One and Number Nine in the workplace can be extremely successful. Their respective skills and talents complement each other well.

The creative flair of Number One is enhanced by the determination and willpower of Number Nine. Number One's desire to succeed no matter what is balanced by Number Nine's compassion and honesty. Together they will probably achieve a great deal and could well go far.

Number One and Number Nine are both strong-willed characters who have a tendency to be confrontational. It would be wise for Number One and Number Nine to avoid becoming locked in petty disputes as this is not the best use of their energy. Number One and Number Nine should allow each other independence and space and should not work together too closely so that they do not spend their time quarrelling.

Once Number One and Number Nine have established their respective roles, they will generally respect and admire each other. Once they get to know each other, Number One and Number Nine may well become good friends outside work.

Romance

A relationship between Number One and Number Nine is likely to be long-lasting and happy. Number One will be attracted to Number Nine's passion and energy, and it is an attraction that will last throughout the relationship.

If Number One is involved with Number Nine, he or she will not find it difficult to prioritize his or her relationship. Number One will be captivated by Number Nine's personality and vitality. Number Nine will also find Number One's ambitious vision attractive. The combination of Number One and Number Nine is electric, and a relationship between these two will be filled with passion.

If Number One does fall into the habit of neglecting his or her partner, it could cause real problems in the relationship. Number Nine needs to have romance and passion in a relationship and if deprived of this by Number One may look elsewhere for excitement.

Number One and Number Nine need to set time aside to spend together so that they can enjoy each other's company. As long as the relationship has equal importance for both, Number One and Number Nine—both individuals—will be happy and they will experience few difficulties.

Birth Date Personality Number Two and Birth Date Personality Number One *see* page 54

Birth Date Personality Number Two and Birth Date Personality Number Two

Work

In the workplace the combination of two Number Twos is not likely to be successful. There is a good chance that two Number Twos will bring out the worst in each other at work.

Number Twos are quiet and reserved characters, and if two Number Twos are working together, neither will want to make decisions or to take on responsibility. The combination of two Number Twos in a working environment could only really work if the two were working together as part of a larger team that included more motivated and ambitious people.

As part of a larger team, their skills are more likely to be obvious and they are more likely to feel content. If recognized, Number Twos may find that their negotiating and compromising skills may result in them playing an important part in the everyday functioning of the team.

Two Number Twos will like each other and get on well in the workplace. In fact, Number Twos will generally be well liked by all their work colleagues because they are unlikely to cause arguments or to ruffle anyone's feathers.

Romance

Two Number Twos are ideally matched in terms of romance. Essentially Number Twos have a need to be fully understood and no one can understand a Number Two better than another Number Two.

In order for Number Two to be happy, he or she needs commitment and stability, and this need will be completely satisfied in a relationship with another Number Two. A relationship between two Number Twos is likely to be a happy and enduring partnership. Once these two have made a commitment to each other, it is unlikely that they will ever part.

The reason that two Number Twos get on so well in a romantic relationship is that they communicate with each other. These two will talk to each other about everything that concerns them and they know that they will be understood. They will respect and admire each other, and they will not tire of each other. Both individuals will feel secure and loved within their relationship together.

Birth Date Personality Number Two and Birth Date Personality Number Three

Work

Number Two and Number Three are likely to work well together as part of a larger team including other more ambitious and responsible people. If Number Two and Number Three work together as a partnership, it is unlikely to succeed because neither is concerned with success or promotion. In a team setting, though, the talents of Number Two and Number Three are more likely to be evident. Number

Two and Number Three are likely to be equally talented and skilful in their work. The work of Number Three, however, is more likely to receive recognition because of Number Three's flamboyant and boastful personality. Number Two is more likely to work away quietly in the background. This could cause some ill-feeling between Number Two and Number Three, although Number Two is unlikely to address the issue. Number Three should recognize that Number Two is working hard and encourage other people to acknowledge Number Two's efforts. This will generally be a harmonious working relationship, with Number Two and Number Three usually getting on well with each other.

Romance
Number Two and Number Three are likely to meet each other at a social function as both enjoy going to parties and gatherings of friends. They are likely to be attracted to each other and a romantic union is probable. The combination of Number Two and Number Three in romantic relationships is generally successful. Number Three likes relationships that are harmonious and Number Two also has a need for harmony— neither is likely to want to argue. Number Three will tend to be slightly more dominant than Number Two in the relationship, and this should be challenged by both Number Two and Number Three. Number Two will put up with a lot for the sake of an easy life and harmony but should be wary of putting up with too much. Number Three should appreciate

the easy-going nature of Number Two and not exploit the situation for his or her own gain.

It is good that both Number Two and Number Three enjoy socializing and that this is an activity that they will do together. Number Three will have fewer opportunities to flirt if Number Two is present and will almost certainly refrain from taking flirtation further if his or her partner is present. Number Three should be careful to limit flirtatious behaviour when Number Two is present as Number Two easily becomes jealous and bitter. Number Two may well view Number Three's flirtation as a form of betrayal and feel that he or she is no longer loved and respected. This is the only area that could cause real problems in an otherwise fortunate match. Number Two and Number Three should discuss this issue and explain their feelings to each other. Number Two will need reassurance from Number Three that there is no threat and Number Two should not try to restrict Number Three's personality.

Birth Date Personality Number Two and Birth Date Personality Number Four

Work

Number Two and Number Four will have a good working relationship. They will get on well together, and their respective skills and talents will be well balanced. Number Four is hard-working and ambitious and will be able to see the potential in Number Two. Number Two's imagination and vision will be the source of inspiration for Number Four, who will be able to turn an idea into a reality. Number Two's negotiating and compromising skills will be required in this working relationship as Number Four is prone to being stubborn and unmoving. Number Four will know where he or she wants to get to and Number Two will know how to work with other people in order to achieve the goal. Number Four's ambition and drive is likely to keep Number Two from becoming pessimistic and disheartened.

Number Four can be quick-tempered and has a tendency to lash out at other people. Number Two is unlikely to fall victim to Number Four's ill-temper as he or she will have noticed the trait and will do everything to avoid a confrontation.

Romance
A relationship between Number Two and Number Four is likely to be a happy and harmonious union. Number Two and Number Four are both looking for commitment and security, and a relationship between these two will probably become serious after a short time. A romance between Number Two and Number Four is unlikely to be a short-lived affair.

Number Two and Number Four will enjoy creating a warm and secure home together. They will spend a great deal of time together planning their future. The key to the happiness of Number Two and Number Four is commitment. Each will know that the other is fully committed to the relationship and, secure in this knowledge, both Number Two and Number Four will thrive. Number Four will learn to be more relaxed and humorous through his or her relationship with Number Two, and Number Two will feel more assertive and able to voice opinions.

Number Two and Number Four will respect and admire each other. Their relationship will be affectionate and loving and will stand the test of time.

Birth Date Personality Number Two and Birth Date Personality Number Five

Work

The combination of Number Two and Number Five in the workplace is unlikely to be successful. The traits that Number Two and Number Five have in common are not traits that will benefit their employers—Number Two and Number Five both lack ambition and a desire for success. Beyond this similarity, Number Two and Number Five have little in common as far as work practices are concerned.

Number Two will be suspicious and wary of Number Five's erratic personality. Number Five is prone to flashes of inspiration and bursts of enthusiasm that can evaporate as quickly as they materialize. Number Five will be keen to work hard on a project for a spate but will tire and will leave the remainder to someone else. Number Two may well find that he or she ends up finishing off a great deal of Number Five's work. Number Two will not appreciate this extra work and responsibility. Number Two may become resentful of Number Five's attitude but is unlikely to challenge it or to present the difficulty to someone else. After a time Number Two may decide not to finish off the work and to become more like Number Five. Number Five, in turn, may lose even sporadic enthusiasm because of Number Two's pessimism. Because of this, Number Two and Number Five can be a bad influence on each other in the workplace. Number Two and Number Five will probably get on well on a personal level and arguments are unlikely, but generally this pair should avoid working together closely.

Romance

Shortly after the initial attraction, Number Two and Number Five may run into difficulties. After a relatively short time, Number Two will indicate that he or she is looking for a long-term relationship and commitment. Number Five will be surprised and wary of this and may be frightened off. Number Two should allow the relationship to progress naturally, without attaching any hopes or expectations to it. Certainly, Number Two should refrain from talking about any expectations that he or she may have of the relationship unless Number Five has in some way indicated an interest in commitment.

If Number Five does feel ready to make a commitment to

Number Two, then Number Two will find that Number Five is a loving and generally faithful partner. Number Two may feel that Number Five's lack of demonstrative affection is a sign that the relationship is not working, but this is just the nature of Number Five and Number Two should accept this. Number Five should try to be more affectionate to Number Two, who really needs a lot of attention and reassurance.

Another area of difficulty is Number Five's flirtatious behaviour. Although this does not mean that Number Five intends to be unfaithful, Number Two will find this behaviour very difficult to handle and become jealous and bitter. Unfortunately, this reaction is likely to result in Number Five becoming tired of the relationship, looking for fun elsewhere and becoming even more flirtatious. If this problem does occur in the relationship, Number Two and Number Five need to talk about it and agree on a way to avoid unhappiness.

With a bit of effort and a lot of communication and understanding, this relationship has the potential to succeed. Certainly, if Number Two and Number Five are able to survive the teething problems of their relationship then it should work out well for both of them.

Birth Date Personality Number Two and Birth date Personality Number Six

Work
The main problem for this pair in the work environment is

lack of ambition and desire for material success. If, however, Number Two and Number Six find themselves working together in a career that does interest them, then their skills and talents will complement each other. Number Six will be able to promote the right image and to generate confidence amongst others. Number Two will be able to use his or her imagination and hard work to achieve the goals. Problems may occur if Number Six takes all the credit for any success, as Number Two may become resentful. Number Six will feel that he or she deserves the attention and recognition because he or she will feel that nothing would have been accomplished without his or her input. Although Number Six may have contributed to the success, it is important that he or she recognizes the efforts of Number Two and realizes that without him or her little would have been achieved.

If Number Two and Number Six find themselves working together in an area that does not interest or motivate them, then they will possibly bring out the worst in each other. Number Six may feel inclined to take advantage of Number Two's easy-going nature, which in turn will make Number Two despondent and pessimistic.

Number Six and Number Two tend to be popular with other people and will probably find that they get on well on a personal level at work. Open arguments and disputes are unlikely between them, but if either is unhappy in the work then under the surface resentments may exist.

Romance

Number Six and Number Two are well matched in terms of romance. Number Two will be open about his or her need for security and commitment and will let Number Six know how she or he is feeling. Number Six will appreciate the honesty of Number Two and will feel secure enough to be able to talk about his or her own emotions. Once commitment has been established, both Number Six and Number Two are likely to be affectionate and loving partners.

Neither Number Six nor Number Two likes to argue or discuss negative feelings, and this could be the source of difficulties in the relationship. Number Six has a tendency to internalize feelings and keep them bottled up, as does Number Two. These negative emotions cannot remain hidden forever and may surface as resentment and discontent generally. Both Number Six and Number Two will want their partner to realize that they are unhappy, although they will not openly say so. Both will become obsessed by their own unhappiness and be unaware of their partner's feelings. Eventually, if these negative feelings are not tackled and resolved, the relationship may break down, and neither Number Six nor Number Two will be able to say exactly why. All this could be avoided by honesty and openness at an early stage. Number Six and Number Two need to communicate with each other and to make a conscious effort to do so. This may be difficult for them, as they both internalize problems and do not like to recognize difficulties. If they do succeed in airing their differences and avoiding the buildup of resentment, they will be very happy together and their relationship will be strong.

Birth Date Personality Number Two and Birth Date Personality Number Seven

Work

If Number Two and Number Seven find themselves working together in an area of work that is concerned with business or finance and is highly competitive, then it is a recipe for disaster. Neither Number Two nor Number Seven has the ambition or desire to thrive in this working environment. They are both very honest and may find that such work challenges their principles. They are also both vague and dreamy and are unlikely to create a favourable impression in a workplace that requires motivation and drive. Alone in such an environment, Number Two may be able to work away in the background, but if working alongside a Number Seven the more relaxed and laidback characteristics of Number Two will become obvious.

Number Two and Number Seven are far more likely to find themselves working together in careers involved with human interest, and in this working environment they will feel more impassioned and committed. If working towards a common and desirable goal, they will work well together and may achieve what they set out to do.

Number Seven and Number Two will like each other very

much as work colleagues and will have a good relationship. In a working environment Number Seven and Number Two will feel that they have found a kindred spirit in each other.

Romance
A relationship between Number Two and Number Seven is likely to become serious very quickly. Both Number Seven and Number Two have a tendency to commit themselves at an early stage in relationships. Number Seven will declare undying love for Number Two, and Number Two will soon voice his or her desire for a lasting and committed relationship. Despite the haste, this pairing is generally very successful. Both Number Seven and Number Two are very affectionate, and both need to feel loved and appreciated. Neither need worry about a lack of affection. Number Two is very supportive and affectionate, and Number Seven is romantic and open with his or her emotions. Both can be insecure in relationships, but this problem is unlikely to surface in this match.

Number Seven is more adventurous than Number Two by nature, but because Number Two feels secure in the relationship, he or she will be willing to go along with Number Seven's plans. The only difficulty that may arise in this relationship is the resolution of any differences of opinion. Both Number Two and Number Seven are stubborn souls and once they make a stand are unlikely to back down. Even the normally compromising Number Two can be steely in his or her determination if absolutely convinced that he or she is in the right. Number Seven and Number Two need to recognize that they occasionally become locked in no-win arguments and should devise a way of coping with this problem. Generally, this will be a harmonious and happy relationship that will bring a great deal of pleasure to both Number Two and Number Seven.

Birth Date Personality Number Two and Birth Date Personality Number Eight

Work

Initially, Number Two may be suspicious and possibly even envious of Number Eight's ambition. After time, however, Number Two will become aware of Number Eight's honesty and integrity. Eventually Number Two will admire Number Eight's ability to work hard and to achieve success without compromising his or her principles. Number Two may well feel inspired by the example of Number Eight and become more motivated and ambitious. Number Eight will recognize the talents and skills of Number Two, and will try to encourage him or her to achieve his or her full potential. Number Eight will gently encourage Number Two to take on more responsibility and to make more decisions. This working relationship has the potential to be very successful. Number Two's ability to compromise and negotiate will balance out Number Eight's tendency to cause confrontations and disputes. If, however, Number Two and Number Eight find themselves in dispute with each other, breaking the deadlock will be no easy task. Once Number Two has decided to make a stance, his or her willpower is an equal match for Number Eight's stubbornness. In this situation they will both need to recognize that they should be working together and that they need to back down in order to achieve their goals. Generally, Number Two and Number Eight will benefit from working together and they will both acquire new skills.

Romance
Although this is not an obviously successful match, it has the potential to succeed. If Number Two and Number Eight find themselves attracted to each other and decide to make a commitment to a relationship together, they will find that although they are quite different their differences will form a good balance. Number Eight's tendency to be reserved and private will be balanced by Number Two's openness and willingness to demonstrate affection. In time Number Eight will feel secure and confident enough to experiment with being open and affectionate. Number Two will appreciate the love and attention of Number Eight once a rapport has been established, and Number Eight will value the support and reassurance provided by Number Two.

Although supportive, Number Two will not fully understand Number Eight's desire for success, and Number Eight should discuss his or her ambitions with Number Two so that he or she can appreciate the importance of success for his or her partner. Number Two and Number Eight will find that communicating with each other is very enjoyable and, over time, will know each other very well.

Difficulties may arise if Number Eight becomes preoccupied with work and material success. Number Two will feel neglected if Number Eight takes to working late and spending more time away from home. Number Eight should recognize the importance of a happy relationship and try to strike a balance between work and home. Number Two should not pressurize Number Eight too much and should acknowledge that Number Eight will occasionally need to put in extra work in order to achieve goals.

A relationship between Number Two and Number Eight will need both individuals to be committed to its success. Once these two get to know each other and find their common ground, they should be happy together and their relationship should be harmonious and secure.

Birth Date Personality Number Two and Birth Date Personality Number Nine

Work

In a working environment Number Two and Number Nine together is a winning combination. Together they strike a good balance and have the potential to succeed. Number Two will instantly be drawn to Number Nine's energy and vitality, and

Number Two will feel inspired. Number Nine will recognize the potential in the ideas and imagination of Number Two, and together they will be able to make them realities. If working with Number Nine, Number Two is likely to find a sense of hope and ambition. Number Two will in no way feel dominated or threatened by Number Nine but will feel that they are working together towards a common goal. Number Nine will benefit from Number Two's ability to negotiate and compromise, which will take the edge of Number Nine's boldness.

Number Two and Number Nine will get on very well as workmates. They both have a keen sense of the importance of fair play and of human rights. They are both compassionate and understanding, and will find that they have a great deal in common. Number Two and Number Nine are likely to become good friends as a result of working together.

Romance

The combination of Number Two and Number Nine is likely to create a joyous union. Number Two and Number Nine are ideally suited to meet each other's needs. Both are very affectionate and loving individuals who are happiest if their love is reciprocated. Both are happy for relationships to become serious after a short time. Indeed, Number Nine needs commitment at an early stage or he or she will look elsewhere. Number Two is more than happy to make an early commitment to a romantic and adoring Number Nine, so this will not be a problem experienced by this pair. In fact, these two individuals will find that they have very few difficulties in their relationship together. Generally, Number Nine and Number Two will find that they have a passionate and romantic relationship that will last a long time.

The only difficulty that may arise is jealousy—both Number Two and Number Nine have a tendency to feel envious of their partner paying attention to another. However, they will not be likely to give each other much cause for jealousy as they generally only have eyes for each other.

Birth Date Personality Number Three and Birth Date Personality Number One *see* **page 56**

Birth Date Personality Number Three and Birth Date Personality Number Two *see* **page 72**

Birth Date Personality Number Three and Birth Date Personality Number Three

Work

Two Number Threes working together is potentially a recipe for disaster. Both individuals are capable of being impetuous, headstrong and reckless. Neither will have the ambition or motivation to succeed at a career, and both will be inclined to cut corners and pay little attention to their work. Number Threes working together will tend to be a bad influence on each other—they will find each other stimulating and interesting and will be far more preoccupied with socializing with each other than with their work, which is likely to take second place. Number Threes have a tendency to be the office clowns, and two Number Threes will be in competition with each other to see who can have the most fun and do the least work. Two Number Threes working together will distract each other and bring out the worst in each other as far as work is concerned.

Two Number Threes will be great friends and will get on brilliantly together. Their colleagues and workmates may be less enthused by this combination.

Romance

There is likely to be a strong and immediate attraction between two Number Threes. They generally will fall into an intense and romantic relationship. Such passion is likely to be short-lived, and both individuals will probably move on to pastures new before too long, as long-term commitment is not a priority for Number Threes. The relationship is not likely to end badly, and they will probably remain good friends.

If two Number Threes are serious about each other and want to make a commitment, then they are well matched in their approach to love. They will find each other's company interesting and stimulating, and will have a natural understanding of each other's needs. Two Number Threes who are committed to each other will share an exciting and passionate relationship that will bring them both a great deal of pleasure. Once a commitment to each other has been made, two Number Threes will embark on adventures as a couple in order to satisfy their need for excitement. A relationship between two Number Threes is likely to be happy and will last for as long as both individuals see fit for it to last.

Birth Date Personality Number Three and Birth Date Personality Number Four

Work

In order for this working relationship to succeed a great deal of time should be spent setting ground rules and getting to know each other. Number Three and Number Four are essentially very different people with different ideas and motivation. Their differences may irritate each other, and they may find it difficult to work together. Number Three may feel that Number Four is slow and unimaginative, and Number Four may feel that Number Three is too reckless and irresponsible. For the sake of their working practices, these two will have to learn to accommodate each other and their differences. Number Four should try to be more relaxed and take more chances, and Number Three should try to be more calm and serious. They should both try to acknowledge each other's strengths and talents and allow each other space and respect.

If in time Number Two and Number Four do work through their differences, they may find that they combine to make a strong partnership if they work together. They may eventually find that they have a lot to learn from each other.

Romance

It is unlikely that Number Three and Number Four will be attracted to each other immediately—they have very different interests and attitudes and share little common ground. Number Three tends to flirt and have brief affairs while Number Four is more interested in settling down.

If Number Three and Number Four do become romantically involved, they will run into difficulties almost immediately. Number Three expects romance and passion and may find Number Four too reserved. Number Four will feel insecure in a relationship with Number Three and will be suspicious and jealous of Number Three flirting with other people. Number Four may attempt to dominate and control Number Three in order to create a relationship that is stable and secure. This, however, is more likely to send Number Three into the arms of another admirer. Number Three is an independent individual who needs space and freedom and will react badly to domineering behaviour.

In order for this relationship to work, both individuals need to be absolutely committed to each other, and they need to be willing to put in a great deal of effort. These two need to communicate with each other and to talk through their emotions. They also need to accommodate each other's differences and accept each other for what he or she is.

Birth Date Personality Number Three and Birth Date Personality Number Five

Work

Initially Number Three and Number Five will work brilliantly together. They both have imagination and vision and the ability to achieve their goals—as long as long-term commitment is not required. Both Number Three and Number Five lack ambition and commitment to work. They are both likely to move on to pastures new after the completion of a particular project. For a short time Number Five will keep Number Three interested in their shared project, and they will encourage each other. They will find each other stimulating to work with and will generate enthusiasm and energy. If Number Three and Number Five find employment that meets their need for change and excitement then their working relationship will last and develop over time.

Even in a short-term project, problems may arise in the working practices of Number Three and Number Five. Both like to take chances and plunge in without much thought and consideration. As neither will raise the issue of caution they may well make hasty and ill-thought-out decisions. Neither Number Three nor Number Five has much interest in finer details. They are both more concerned with the larger picture and the end result. To function at their best, this pair would benefit from working in a team that contained more cautious and practical individuals.

Romance

Number Three and Number Five will be instantly attracted to each other. They are both flirtatious by nature and they will enjoy each other's company. If the initial flirtation develops into a more serious relationship they may experience some difficulties. The main problem for Number Three will be Number Five's apparent lack of attention. In order to get a reaction from Number Five, Number Three may flirt with other people. Rather than become jealous Number Five may well do just the same, which will deeply hurt Number Three and seemingly confirm his or her fears that Number Five simply does not care. Neither is suited to difficult relationships and both tend to move on to avoid problems.

In order for this relationship to work both Number Three and Number Five will need to talk about their feelings and be open with each other. They will need to understand each other and Number Three will need reassurance and affection. If Number Three and Number Five put in the effort there is a fair chance that the relationship will succeed. How long the relationship lasts really depends on the level of commitment of the two individuals involved.

Birth Date Personality Number Three and Birth Date Personality Number Six

Work

Neither Number Three nor Number Six has a strong sense of

ambition or a desire to take on the responsibility of making decisions. Number Three and Number Six have similar personalities, and these personalities are not particularly suited to working environments. Both have a tendency to be lazy and both lack motivation for work. Another trait common to both Number Three and Number Six is drifting. Both tend to spend short periods of time in one form of employment before drifting off to start afresh in a new job. They tend to move on once any difficulties begin to manifest themselves.

Number Three is the more creative of this pair and Number Six is more talented at presentation. If they can somehow find a project that interests them both and about which they are both enthusiastic then they do have the skills and talents to do well. Finding a career that suits Number Three and Number Six is the biggest obstacle in their way. Once they have found a common goal they will work well together. Number Three and Number Six will like each other and get on well as colleagues. This is very important for both Number Three and Number Six because, for both of them, contentment and happiness is of utmost importance. Number Three and Number Six would not put up with disharmony in the workplace.

Romance

Number Three and Number Six are both attractive individuals. The attraction of Number Six to Number Three will be his or her ability to project the right image and stand out from the crowd. Number Six will be attracted to Number Three's openness and childlike charms.

Once a relationship between these two has been established it will become apparent that Number Three expects more attention and romance from Number Six than Number Six is prepared to give. Number Three has high expectations of relationships and requires romance and excitement to remain committed to his or her partner. If Number Six does not respond to Number Three's needs then Number Three may well look elsewhere for excitement. Number Three is a natural flirt and will have no difficulty in attracting a string of admirers.

Number Six will be aware of Number Three's discontent and of the fact that Number Three is flirting with others. Number Six will be hurt by his or her partner's actions but will not risk a confrontation. He or she is more likely to internalize his or her disappointment and jealousy. This will ultimately make Number Six very unhappy and the relationship could be in jeopardy.

In order for Number Three and Number Six to form a successful and happy relationship they need to be realistic about their expectations of each other. They should be open and honest about what they want from a relationship and from each other. If Number Three and Number Six are open with each other and talk through any difficulties they will have a successful relationship. They have similar personalities, share many interests and generally get on very well together.

Birth Date Personality Number Three and Birth Date Personality Number Seven

Work

Number Three and Number Seven have got a lot to gain from working together. They have a lot that they can teach each other. Number Three has energy and inspiration, which if incorporated by Number Seven will enhance his or her work, and Number Seven has wisdom and understanding, which can be lacking in the work of Number Three but if implemented by Number Three could make his or her work more steady and reliable. A good balance is struck between Number Three and Number Seven in terms of a working relationship. Their skills and talents complement each other and their negative traits cancel each other out. Number Three can tend to be impulsive and act without much thought or concern for the outcome. Number Seven's careful and considerate approach will challenge Number Three's practice and mistakes may be avoided. In turn Number Seven can be indecisive and lacking in vision but Number Three's energy and decisiveness will counteract this.

The only difficulty that may arise in this working relationship is if both Number Three and Number Seven simultaneously give in to the more vague and dreamy side of their characters. If this happens they may temporarily get distracted from what they are meant to be doing. This is not, however, likely to cause any profound problems.

Both Number Three and Number Seven will need to feel committed to their work in order for them to succeed. Neither will be prepared to put in hard work for a project that they don't believe in. Once working in the right environment, Number Three and Number Seven will work very well together. They will respect and like each other and will probably be good friends as well as colleagues. Number Three and Number Seven will understand each other and will allow each other space and independence.

Romance

Generally this is a very fortunate match. Number Three and Number Seven are well suited in terms of a romantic relationship. After the initial attraction it will not be long before this pair become serious about each other. Number Seven will typically fall head over heals in love with Number Three, and it is this sort of obvious display of passion and love that Number Three thrives on. Number Three will be more than happy to return the attentions of Number Seven, and they will have a very romantic relationship.

The only real difficulty that this couple is likely to experience will arise through their difference in attitude towards social events. Number Three lives for social interaction and will want to make the most of every invitation. Number Seven, on the other hand, is a more private person and less likely to enjoy a hectic social life. This difference in attitude may result in Number Three attending social functions alone. The danger here is that Number Three will have the opportunity to flirt. Number Seven could become quite insecure and jealous if Number Three is out with other people most of the time.

To avoid such difficulties, Number Three and Number Seven should try to compromise and strike a balance between socializing and spending time alone together. If they are able to manage their spare time so that they are both happy, then they are likely to be enamoured with each other for a long time. There will be a dreamlike quality about their relationship. They will have few quarrels as neither is argumentative by nature.

Birth Date Personality Number Three and Birth Date Personality Number Eight

Work
The combination of Number Three's ability to communicate and Number Eight's business sense is a recipe for success for this working partnership. Number Three and Number Eight work well together and bring out the best in each other. The ambition and enthusiasm of Number Eight are a good influences on Number Three, who, after interacting with Number Eight, will feel more motivated and determined. Number Eight will recognize Number Three's skills and his or her ability to communicate. Number Eight will encourage Number Three to make the

most of his or her talents. Number Eight will be able to organize and focus Number Three without Number Three feeling controlled or imposed upon. Number Three will respect and like Number Eight and will want to create a good impression. Number Three's adaptability will impress Number Eight, and Number Eight will recognize the need to give Number Three variety in his or her work. Together Number Three and Number Eight will be able to establish the roles that they are happiest working in. Generally, Number Three will work with people and Number Eight will manage the practicalities.

This is likely to be a successful and long-lasting working relationship. Number Three is less likely to change careers if he or she is working closely with Number Eight.

Romance

Number Three and Number Eight are not an obvious match in terms of romance. There is unlikely to be much in the way of initial attraction between these two.

If Number Three and Number Eight do get together they will run into difficulties at an early stage. Number Three will not be impressed by Number Eight's lack of attention and reluctance to be open emotionally. Generally, Number Eight is not romantic or passionate enough to satisfy Number Three. There is a strong possibility that Number Three will look for excitement and passion with someone else before too long. Number Three will not play second fiddle to Number Eight's career, and Number Eight's ambitions will seem irrelevant to Number Three.

Number Eight will not receive the understanding and support that he or she needs from Number Three. Number Three will not want to discuss career matters, and Number Eight will feel neglected and unappreciated. Number Eight will not tolerate infidelities, and if Number Three is having an affair then Number Eight will call off the romance.

In order for this relationship to succeed, both individuals need to be completely committed to each other and really want to be together. They will need to spend a lot of time talking about their individual needs and expectations. They will have to make allowances for each other's needs and for each other's limitations. They will have to accept each other for what they are and learn how to make each other happy.

Birth Date Personality Number Three and Birth Date Personality Number Nine

Work

Number Three and Number Nine are very similar in many ways. They are both drifters who experience short bursts of enthusiasm. Both Number Nine and Number Three have a tendency to chop and change their careers at regular intervals. Neither really has the motivation or determination to stay in one position for any length of time.

If Number Three and Number Nine's career paths do cross,

they will enjoy working together. Number Three and Number Nine both have wonderful imaginations and great vision. They will bounce ideas off each other and come up with bigger and better plans. The down side to their work practice is that neither has any interest in the practicalities or minor points involved in a project and both are likely to lose interest after the conception of the plan. They are both risk takers and not given to assessing the feasibility of their ideas. They may well encourage each other to take greater and greater risks as neither will suggest being cautious. For these reasons Number Three and Number Nine work best together as part of a larger team that includes more cautious individuals and people who are concerned with details and practicalities. It is in this sort of working environment that they are most likely to flourish.

Number Three and Number Nine will get on well with each other as colleagues. Indeed, they are more than likely to become good friends on a personal level as well. Eventually they may both drift off to new careers but they are likely to remain friends.

Romance
There will be an instant attraction between Number Three and Number Nine. Both Number Nine and Number Three are likely to stand out from the crowd at a social event, and they will be attracted to each other for this reason.

Once Number Three and Number Nine have established a

relationship, they will find themselves on a romantic roller-coaster. They will have a passionate and intensely romantic relationship that will be fast-moving and highly charged. Such is the intensity of a relationship between these two that even the most fickle Number Three will not feel the need to look elsewhere for excitement. Number Three and Number Nine are unlikely to ever tire of each other or find each other dull. They both have impetuous and impulsive natures, which will ensure that there is always a spark in their lives together. They will be completely committed to each other and will be absolutely secure in each other's love.

The problems that this couple are likely to encounter will not be with each other but with their finances. Both have a lack of understanding about financial matters and neither would want to spoil an adventure by considering their ability to afford it. For these reasons, there is a fair chance that this pair could end up owing money for luxuries they can't afford. Even in poverty and debt these two will be happy together, but it would be better if they could occasionally spare a thought for their bank balance.

Once Number Nine and Number Three have found love together they are more than likely to spend the rest of their lives together. They will certainly make each other very happy for the time that they are together.

Birth Date Personality Number Four and Birth Date Personality Number One *see* **page 58**

Birth Date Personality Number Four and Birth Date Personality Number Two *see* page 74

Birth Date Personality Number Four and Birth Date Personality Number Three *see* page 89

Birth Date Personality Number Four and Birth Date Personality Number Four

Work

Both individuals are completely committed to succeeding in their chosen careers. In order to achieve their ambitions both Number Fours know that they have to be practical and reasonable. Both share the ability to work through any problem that may present itself. The key to success for two Number Fours is combining the ability to compromise and listen with strong will and determination. Another skill that Number Fours possess is being able to learn from previous mistakes, which is invaluable. One Number Four usually has enough potential to make success a strong possibility but for two Number Fours working together success is practically guaranteed.

Two Number Fours will completely understand each other in the working environment. They will both recognize the importance of working together and not trying to compete with each other. Other people may find Number Fours too harsh and ambitious, but for two Number Fours this will be grounds for respect and admiration. There is no doubt that two Number Fours working together will get things done.

Romance

The combination of two fours in a romantic relationship is likely to be successful. They will fully appreciate and understand each other's need to succeed in his or her chosen career and will not try to stand in each other's way. They will respect and admire each other and will happy and secure together.

Two Number Fours will enjoy a happy home life together. They will enjoy spending their free time creating the right home environment. Together they will furnish their home with the best quality furniture and equipment. The home of two Number Fours is likely to be the envy of their friends.

Two Number Fours may argue with each other occasionally. Arguments are especially likely if one or both is experiencing stress at work, as both tend to take out their frustrations on their partner. This will not cause any real problems, however, because they have a unique understanding of each other and they will both realise that the arguments are not related to their partnership.

A relationship between two Fours is likely to be long-lasting and extremely happy. Neither is particularly emotional or romantic, but they will respect, understand and love each other in their own special way.

Birth Date Personality Number Four and Birth Date Personality Number Five

Work

Number Four and Number Five could hardly be more different in their approach to work. Number Four is clearly career-minded and determined to be successful, but Number Five has no real interest in careers or success.

It will take a long time for Number Four and Number Five to establish any sort of working relationship. Initially Number Four and Number Five will probably avoid working together while they try to understand what makes each other tick. Number Four will find it very difficult to understand Number Five. Number Four will probably find it hard to believe that anyone can be so lacking in ambition as Number Five. Number Five in turn will find the concept of being focused entirely on career success completely alien. Number Five will, however, be fascinated by Number Four and will want to form a working relationship in order to get to know him or her better.

If Number Four and Number Five do get to know each other and find that they can work together then they may well learn a lot from each other. Number Four could benefit from learning to be more adaptable and easy-going, and this is Number Five's area of expertise. Number Five would definitely benefit from being more focused and ambitious, and Number Four will be able to be a positive influence in this area. The key to success for this working partnership is acknowledging and respecting each other's differences and not trying to impose on each other.

Romance

Number Four and Number Five have very different expectations of romantic relationships. Number Five is essentially looking for a good time and the opportunity to meet lots of different people. Number Four, on the other hand, is looking for long-term commitment with someone suitable. It is hard to imagine an initial attraction between these two because they are so different but on occasion opposites do attract. The most likely scenario is Number Five making the first move in an attempt to widen his or her social circle. Number Four may be flattered by Number Five's attention and may feel that Number Five is in need of a stable influence in his or her life.

If a relationship between Number Four and Number Five develops, then they will experience a few difficulties. One of the biggest problems will be Number Four's desire to control his or her partner. Number Five in no way wants to be restricted or dominated and may react very badly to any attempts by Number Four to impose his or her will. The most likely reaction from an unhappy Number Five is to walk away and start anew elsewhere. Number Four should try to allow his or her partner more freedom and accept him or her for what he or she is.

Another problem is Number Five's inability to control his or her finances. Number Five is likely to be reckless with money and to squander it on frivolous objects or on a flutter on the horses. Number Four will be appalled by Number Five's lack of respect for money and will not be able to contain his or her anger. Number Four is more likely than not to be the person in the relationship who earns more money and will feel that Number Five has no right to waste it. Number Five will see Number Four's concerns about finances as dull and unimportant and just another attempt to spoil his or her fun. Number Five should try to be more considerate of Number Four's feelings and act a little less selfishly.

In order for this relationship to work, both individuals will need to put in a great deal of effort. They will have to recognize their differences and accept that these are what they love about each other.

Birth Date Personality Number Four and Birth Date Personality Number Six

Work
Number Four and Number Six will find that they are able to work well together. Number Four's determination and hard work will be enhanced by Number Six's ability to promote and present things in the right light. Number Four and Number Six are both deeply practical individuals and

will be completely committed to doing whatever is necessary to complete their joint task. Number Six is more skilled at dealing with people than Number Four, and his or her ability to compromise and negotiate will be a good balance to Number Four's occasional selfishness and stubbornness.

Number Four and Number Six will have a great deal of respect for each other and will acknowledge their respective areas of expertise. Number Four and Number Six also share a belief in traditional ways and the status quo, which will probably unite them as friends as well as colleagues.

Problems may arise in this working relationship if Number Six gives in to the more lazy and less motivated side of his or her character. Number Four may well become resentful if he or she feels that Number Six is just putting the icing on the cake while he or she does all the hard work. Number Four could also have cause for resentment if Number Six receives all the credit and recognition for their combined efforts. Number Six is likely to be noticed because he or she will be involved in the promotional side of the project. Rather than just accepting all the praise, Number Six should point out that Number Four put in a lot of hard work. As long as there is a fair balance of work and recognition in this working relationship, both Number Four and Number Six will be happy.

Romance

Number Four and Number Six are likely to be attracted to each other because of their shared interest in traditional ways. Once they get to know each other, they will find that they have a great deal in common and that they both have a basically practical approach to life. Both Number Four and Number Six will be happy to make a commitment to each other and will take their responsibility to each other very seriously. Number Four and Number Six are both very faithful individuals and infidelity is most unlikely to be a problem in this relationship.

Neither Number Four nor Number Six is particularly comfortable about expressing emotions. They will not be impulsively passionate or romantic on a regular basis. This is not an indication that they do not care for each other, and they will express their love and devotion in other ways. Occasions such as anniversaries and birthdays are likely to be seen by Number Four and Number Six as being suitable opportunities to be romantic. A union between Number Four and Number Six is not likely to be an intensely passionate one, but it will be happy and a source of security and joy for both individuals.

If Number Four and Number Six do experience any difficulties in their relationship, these will not take the form of raging arguments. Number Six will do anything to avoid confrontation and will not allow an argument to begin. Number Four is more prone to display ill-temper and may well be irritable and snappy with his or her partner. Number Six will see that this is just in Number Four's nature and let the scene pass without comment. Number Four should not take advantage of Number Six's nature and should avoid becoming a bully.

Birth Date Personality Number Four and Birth Date Personality Number Seven

Work

Number Four and Number Seven have a great deal in common in terms of their working practices. Both Number Four and Number Seven are hard-working and reliable individuals who have the ability to get the job in hand done. They are both completely honest and trustworthy and share a mutual respect for the work ethic. The talents and characteristics that Number Four and Number Seven have in common could form the basis of a very successful working relationship.

There are differences between Number Four and Number Seven, though, and these differences could prove to be significant. Number Four is very traditional in his or her approach to life and is naturally distrustful of anyone who challenges the norm. Number Seven is likely to be unconventional, and his or her alternative approach to life may be a source of offence for Number Four. Number Four will probably not let his or her prejudices interfere with work, however, and in time will learn to accept Number Seven. Number Seven lacks confidence in communicating and working with people so Number Four will need to fully utilize his or her own abilities in this area to compensate for Number Seven. Number Four will also need to take the lead in making decisions and delegating tasks as Number Seven will probably be daunted by responsibility.

Because Number Seven is not obviously strong-willed, Number Four may occasionally get a bit carried away with his or her power and try to boss Number Seven around. Number Seven will not appreciate this as he or she is a very independent individual. Number Seven has the capability of being just as stubborn and unmoving as Number Four, and they may well find themselves in deadlock situations from time to time. Number Four will have more respect for Number Seven once this side of his or her character becomes obvious, and disputes may well strengthen this working partnership.

Romance
If Number Four and Number Seven find themselves romantically involved with each other, the chances are that their relationship will become a serious commitment before long. Number Seven will probably fall head over heals in love with Number Four and declare undying devotion. Number Four will be flattered and will no doubt suggest making the relationship more official. This process of making a long-term

commitment to each other may happen over a very short time and may in fact be too quick. Number Four and Number Seven should try to put on the brakes a little and think seriously about their compatibility and their future together before becoming too involved.

If Number Four and Number Seven do decide to go ahead and make a commitment to each other, they will generally be happy together. Number Seven is a very open and emotional individual who will constantly reassure Number Four of his or her love. Number Four is not naturally confident about discussing affairs of the heart but may feel so secure in Number Seven's love that he or she is willing to open up. If Number Four is not open with Number Seven, Number Seven may become insecure and doubt that he or she is loved by his or her partner. Number Four should try to find a way to express emotions and Number Seven should accept that not everyone is as able to be open emotionally.

There is a danger in this relationship that Number Four will try to be the dominant partner and impose his or her will on Number Seven. Number Seven will rebel against any attempts at control by Number Four. Number Four should avoid adopting a domineering role, or real problems could arise in the relationship.

Number Four and Number Seven will generally be happy together and their relationship should stand the test of time. Their relationship would be strengthened if they find leisure interests that they can share.

Birth Date Personality Number Four and Birth Date Personality Number Eight

Work

The combination of Number Four and Number Eight together in the workplace is a recipe for success. They have a great deal in common and share deep ambition and a determination to do well in their chosen careers. Both are prepared to put in the necessary hard work to achieve the goals that they set themselves. Number Four and Number Eight will each recognize that the other has all the most admirable qualities that can be found in a colleague. Both have respect for reliable, practical and rational individuals, as, indeed, that is what they both are. The key to the success of the working relationship between Number Four and Number Eight is that they are able to trust each other to work independently. They do not doubt each other's ability to assess situations and make decisions on the spot. Additionally, as well as allowing each other the space to work independently, they are able to work well together as a team.

It is not only positive characteristics that Number Four and Number Eight have in common. They also share a tendency to be stubborn and uncompromising. There is a strong possibility that if these two disagree with each other they could become locked in dispute. Both are too practical to let any dispute get to the point that it affects their work and they will find a way to resolve their differences. Number Four is more likely to see the opportunity for compromise than Number Eight, who has a strong conviction that he or she is never wrong. Number Four has more humility and is better able to learn from his or her mistakes. Number Eight would do well to try to learn from Number Four's example.

Generally, Number Four and Number Eight will get on well with each other as colleagues. Their working relationship will probably last a long time and bring them both a great many rewards.

Romance

Number Four and Number Eight are well suited to each other in terms of romance. They both have a similar approach to life and share many of the same attitudes. They are both ambitious and wish to do well in life. If these two meet each other at a social function they will spend a great deal of time talking to each other and will feel that they have found their soul mate. Once they have discovered each other, they are not likely to let each other go and will make sure that they see each other again.

There is little doubt that Number Four and Number Eight are suited to making a long-term commitment to each other. They will understand each other and be able to offer each other support and affection. Careers are equally important to Number Four and Number Eight, and they will be happy to allow each other time and space to fulfil their ambitions. Both will find it rewarding to have a partner with whom they are able to share their hopes and discuss their dreams.

The relationship between Number Four and Number Eight will not be particularly passionate or romantic but will be loving and caring. Number Four and Number Eight will both feel extremely secure and happy in their relationship and they will probably stay together for a long time.

Birth Date Personality Number Four and Birth Date Personality Number Nine

Work

Number Four and Number Nine are very different individuals. Number Four is a practical and careful traditionalist. Number Nine is bold, flighty and unconventional. Number Four and Number Nine have a great deal that they could learn from each other. If they are able to be open with each other, they have a lot to gain from the experience of working together. Number Four could benefit from learning to take more risks and being more adaptable and imaginative. These are Number Nine's areas of expertise and Number Nine would be happy to share his or her skills. Number Two in turn could benefit from Number Four's practical skills and ability to stop and think before acting. If they can recognize and respect each other's skill and talents, this working partnership will have the ability to go far.

Unfortunately, it is more likely that Number Four and

Number Nine will remain closed to one another. They will probably both be distrustful and suspicious of someone so different from themselves. They will generally not have the time to get to know each other well enough to benefit from working together. Number Four and Number Nine will tend to avoid each other in the workplace and will not realize that they are missing a valuable opportunity to develop their own work practices.

Romance

Number Four and Number Nine have very different expectations of romantic relationships and completely different ways of expressing their emotions. Number Nine expects fireworks and passion from a relationship and expresses himself or herself openly. Number Four is more quiet and reserved and has an expectation that relationships will develop into long-term commitments.

Despite their obvious differences, Number Four and Number Nine are well matched in terms of romance. This is definitely a case of opposites attracting. The energy and passion of Number Nine will inspire Number Four to be more free with his or her emotions. Number Four will discover a side to his or her character that he or she did not know existed. Number Nine will be flattered by Number Four's devotion and will feel secure. Number Nine will feel able to make a commitment to Number Four and be happy to spend more time at home.

Problems may arise if Number Four starts to be ill-tempered towards Number Nine. Number Nine will be completely surprised by Number Four's bursts of anger and will not know how to handle the situation. Number Four should be careful not to dominate or control Number Nine, who will tolerate any form of inequality in the relationship.

Generally, Number Four and Number Nine will have few problems and will be happy together. The relationship between Number Four and Number Nine should be long-lasting and harmonious.

Birth Date Personality Number Five and Birth Date Personality Number One *see* page 60

Birth Date Personality Number Five and Birth Date Personality Number Two *see* page 76

Birth Date Personality Number Five and Birth Date Personality Number Three *see* page 91

Birth Date Personality Number Five and Birth Date Personality Number Four *see* page 104

Birth Date Personality Number Five and Birth Date Personality Number Five

Work
The combination of two Number Fives in the workplace should be avoided wherever possible. These two will be a

disruptive influence on each other and on anyone who is trying to work in the same place as them. Two Number Fives will share a tendency to avoid responsibility and hard work, which means that someone else will have to make up their shortfalls. Neither of these two individuals will be ambitious or have any commitment to the work that they are employed to do. Both are likely to be poor timekeepers and to be easily distracted throughout their working day. Number Fives do not like other people imposing restrictions on them, and these two will encourage each other to rebel against any form of authority that they can identify. Neither of these individuals is really suited to the working environment, but having two Number Fives together could create chaos. Their lack of commitment and inability to comply with rules and standards could have a disruptive influence on even the most hard-working employee. Number Fives will do anything to distract people from their work in order to have fun.

For the above reasons, these two individuals will find themselves looking for new employment before long. Disruptive behaviour is likely to be noticed and the responsible individuals disciplined. Number Fives are not likely to want to stay at a place of work where they have been reprimanded. It would be better for Number Fives not to work together but they enjoy themselves together so much that they will be tempted to stay working together.

Romance

A romance between two Number Fives is more likely than not to take the form of a brief affair rather than a long-term commitment. Number Fives tend to drift from one relationship to another with ease. Number Fives are not too keen on commitment.

If two Number Fives do feel that they would like to make a commitment to each other, then there is a fair chance that they will find happiness together. Two Number Fives would share a sense of adventure and a fondness for active lifestyles, and it is their common interests that will unite them. It may well be that two Number Fives feel that, romantically speaking, their wandering days are over and that they would like to find a partner to share their future adventures. In these circumstances two Number Fives will be happy together and they will enjoy a caring and supportive relationship. Neither individual will be particularly demonstrative but both will know that they are loved.

Two Number Fives are well matched for romance and will be happy together. They will remain together for whatever length of time suits them.

Birth Date Personality Number Five and Birth Date Personality Number Six

Work

Number Six and Number Five are very different individuals with different approaches to work. Sometimes people with different personalities can bring out the best in each other and form a great working relationship. This is not the case for Number Five and Number Six. Number Five will be keen to have fun and cause disruptions in the workplace while Number Six will just want a quiet life and harmonious surroundings. Number Six will be concerned with projecting a positive image of the work force whereas Number Five will be constantly challenging the status quo.

Number Five and Number Six do have certain characteristics in common, but these are not ones that are likely to produce a successful working partnership. Number Five and Number Six are both self-contained and have no real interest in learning from other people. Number Five and Number Six are likely to be content with the way that they work and will largely avoid any contact with each other. Neither Number Five nor Number Six is particularly concerned with doing well in his or her chosen career and will have no burning ambitions.

Working together will have no real impact on the lives the two. It will be an unmemorable event for both of them.

Romance
Number Five is likely to find Number Six attractive because of his or her ability to stand out from the crowd. Number Five will be determined to get to know Number

Six better and will arrange a future meeting. Number Six should be wary of having too high expectations of a union with Number Five. Number Five will probably just be looking for a brief affair rather than any form of commitment. There is a strong possibility that Number Six could be hurt by Number Five and feel rejected if Number Five drifts off. Number Six should think very carefully before becoming involved with Number Five.

Number Five and Number Six are not really very compatible in terms of romance. Number Five is unpredictable and alternative, and Number Six is far more traditional. Number Six may well begin to feel out of his or her depth if he or she tries to keep up with Number Five. Number Five is constantly on the lookout for change and excitement, which goes against the grain for Number Six who needs harmony and stability. Number Six should not allow himself or herself to be at the mercy of Number Five's whims but should be more assertive about his or her own needs. Number Six should be aware that a relationship with Number Five holds no guarantee of lasting and should be prepared for disappointment.

A relationship between Number Five and Number Six should be approached lightly by both individuals. They should enjoy it while it lasts and not have too many expectations of each other.

Birth Date Personality Number Five and Birth Date Personality Number Seven

Work

Number Five and Number Seven are not likely to have a particularly good working relationship. The only thing that Number Five and Number Seven have in common is a lack of ambition. Other than that, their approaches to work are completely different.

Number Seven is hard-working and reliable. Number Five is workshy and unreliable. There is a danger that Number Seven will end up working harder than necessary to make up for Number Five's lack of effort. Number Five is not malicious but has no work ethic and will do as little as he or she possibly can. Number Seven will be offended if he or she feels that Number Five is taking advantage of his or her good nature. This sort of injustice will be commented on by Number Seven, who will certainly challenge Number Five and may even take it to Number Five's superior. Number Five will be likely to move on to another job if life is made difficult for him or her by Number Seven.

In order for Number Five and Number Seven to work together well, Number Five will need to be more responsible and Number Seven should avoid taking on Number Five's workload as well as his or her own. If Number Seven does not try to compensate for Number Five's lack of effort, then Number Five will not be able to take advantage of Number

Seven and they will enjoy a more harmonious working relationship.

Romance

Number Five and Number Seven may well find themselves attracted to each other when they first meet. If they decide that they want to get to know each other better then a romance may quickly develop.

Number Seven should be cautious about becoming involved with Number Five. There is a good chance that Number Seven could be hurt and disappointed as a result of an involvement with Number Five. Number Five and Number Seven have very different attitudes towards relationships. Number Five is only really interested in brief affairs with no real commitment whereas Number Seven is looking for everlasting love. Number Seven may fall in love with Number Five and express his or her desire to make the relationship more permanent. Number Five may well be frightened off by Number Seven's need for commitment and Number Seven could be left feeling rejected.

If Number Seven does meet a Number Five who shares his or her desire for commitment, then there is a fair chance that the relationship will be successful. There will, however, be some differences that Number Five and Number Seven will need to resolve before they can be truly happy together. Number Seven is a naturally demonstrative person who has no difficulty in expressing emotions. Number Five is not particularly demonstrative, but when he or she does express feelings he or she is completely sincere. Number Seven should appreciate this about Number Five and should not doubt Number Five's love because he or she does not declare it constantly. Number Five should be aware that Number Seven will be unhappy if he or she is openly flirtatious with other people, and Number Five should try to be considerate of Number Seven's feelings.

Once Number Five and Number Seven have worked through their difficulties and are established in a relationship together, they will generally be happy together. If both individuals are equally committed to the success of the relationship it will last for a long time.

Birth Date Personality Number Five and Birth Date Personality Number Eight

Work
Number Five and Number Eight will enjoy a good working relationship with each other. Number Eight's ambition and practical skills will be enhanced by Number Five's imagination and vision.

Number Eight will instantly recognize the potential that exists within Number Five, and Number Eight will encourage Number Five to make the most of his or her abilities. Number Five will be flattered by the attentions of Number Eight and will want to live up to his or her expectations.

Number Five will feel motivated and inspired by Number Eight's attitude and will find new talents. Number Eight will have the right approach to working with Number Five. He or she will not try to impose his or her will on Number Five but will allow Number Five the space and freedom to be creative. As a result, Number Eight will benefit from Number Five working at his or her optimum level. Number Five's creativity and vision will be enhanced and will sparkle and shine to Number Eight's work.

The working relationship between Number Five and Number Eight will be successful but not long-lasting. It is not in Number Five's nature to stay in one place for any length of time and he or she will move on before long. Number Eight will accept this and will also be able to move on.

Romance

A romance between Number Five and Number Eight is not likely to be a serious affair. They will probably not be that serious about each other. If any long-lasting relationship develops between Number Five and Number Eight it will take a long time to get off the ground.

Initially, Number Five will be attracted to Number Eight's determination and energy and will want to get to know him or her and understand his or her motivation. Number Eight may well be flattered by Number Five's attentions but be unwilling to make any sort of commitment to Number Five before he or she knows what Number Five's intentions are.

Number Five will probably be unwilling to make a commitment, and the relationship may fizzle out at this point. However, Number Five may find himself or herself fascinated by Number Eight and decide to make a go of the relationship. In this case Number Five and Number Eight will probably be very happy together. They will probably live independent lives but will be content as long as they are both sure of the other's commitment.

Birth Date Personality Number Five and Birth Date Personality Number Nine

Work

Number Five and Number Nine will form a powerfully energetic and imaginative working partnership. Together Number Five and Number Nine will make great plans and have fantastic vision. They will be a source of inspiration to each other.

Number Five has a tendency to lose the plot and go off-course. This will be kept in check by Number Nine's ability to work under pressure. In order to meet deadlines, Number Nine will insist that attention needs to be focused on the job in hand. Number Five may be reluctant to take on responsibility, but Number Nine will be more than happy to shoulder total responsibility.

Number Nine and Number Five are well suited to working together. There are few people with whom Number Five could work for a long time but Number Nine is definitely someone who will fit the bill. Number Nine is the ideal working partner for Number Five. Easy-going but full of energy and inspiration, Number Nine will be able to create the right working environment for Number Five to thrive in. If working with Number Nine, Number Five may decide that he or she has found a job that he or she can stick with.

Romance

A brief but passionate affair between Number Five and Number Nine is the most likely scenario. Both Number Five and Number Nine are better suited to short-term romances than long-term commitment. There will be no ill-feeling but both individuals will probably move on to pastures new before long.

If Number Five and Number Nine do feel that they have reached a point in their lives where they would like to make a commitment, then they will find that they are well suited to each other. They will find each other interesting and exciting, and they will lead an adventurous life together. Number Nine is by far the more passionate and demonstrative of the pair and will encourage Number Five to be more free with his or her emotions. Number Nine will be impressed by Number Five's sincerity and will be touched when Number Five does declare his or her love.

Number Five and Number Nine will experience few difficulties in their life together. Both are easy-going by nature and neither has an interest in arguing for the sake of it. They will undoubtedly be happy together but the duration of their relationship really depends on their willingness to settle down.

Birth Date Personality Number Six and Birth Personality Number One *see* page 62

Birth Date Personality Number Six and Birth Personality Number Two *see* page 78

Birth Date Personality Number Six and Birth Personality Number Three *see* page 92

Birth Date Personality Number Six and Birth Personality Number Four *see* page 106

Birth Date Personality Number Six and Birth Personality Number Five *see* page 118

Birth Date Personality Number Six and Birth Personality Number Six

Work
If working together in the right environment, the skills and talents of two Number Sixes will combine to strengthen each individual's existing creativity and imagination. Two Number

Sixes are best suited to working together in a field of work that requires the talents that they have. They will probably find themselves working together in areas such as advertising, fashion design, interior design, etc. In these areas of work they will flourish and be highly regarded.

If two Number Sixes find themselves working together in an environment that does not suit their personalities, they will be a bad influence on each other. There is a real possibility that if working in the wrong environment one Number Six will lose motivation but if two Number Sixes are united in their discontent they may become actively lazy. If working together but not feeling appreciated, the usually communicative and tactful Number Sixes may choose just to exclude other workers and stick together. In these circumstances both Number Sixes should look for new employment in a field that interests them.

Romance
There will be an instant attraction between two Number Sixes. They will probably both be the centre of attention at a social function and will be impressed by each other's ability to present the right image for the occasion.

The chances are that for two Number Sixes an initial attraction will develop into a more serious relationship. Once they get to know each other, both Number Sixes will be pleased to discover that they have found a kindred spirit in each other. They will find that they have a natural and instinctive understanding for what the other is feeling, and the communication problems that Number Six can experience with other people will not be an issue in this relationship. Two Number Sixes will be relaxed in each other's company and will be happy to experiment with being more open with their feelings.

Two Number Sixes will have a beautiful home, and they will spend a lot of time together there. They will have a happy and harmonious relationship and will stay together for a long time.

Birth Date Personality Number Six and Birth Date Personality Number Seven

Work

Number Six and Number Seven are very different individuals and they have little in common. The experience of working together will be of little value to either individual. They will not really learn anything new from each other as they will not be willing to get to know each other.

Number Seven is quiet and introspective. He or she will be lost in his or her own thoughts while he or she gets on with the job in hand. He or she will not be impressed by Number Six's ability to present the right image, and Number Six will resent Number Seven's lack of respect for his or her talents. Number Seven may notice that Number Six has a tendency to do less than his or her fair share of the work and may present this opinion to Number Six, who will be further infuriated. Number Six needs harmonious surroundings and covers over cracks rather than cause discord. Number Seven, however, feels that irregularities need to be challenged and will feel the need to rock the boat if things are not as they should be. This basic difference in attitude could make Number Six most unhappy, and he or she may look elsewhere for employment.

Number Six and Number Seven will probably not work well together and should try to avoid working together too closely. If they do find themselves working together, they should allow each other respect and independence and give each other plenty of space.

Romance

Number Seven is an unlikely target for the attentions of Number Six. Number Seven is too quiet and withdrawn for Number Six, who is looking for someone who stands out from the crowd. Likewise, Number Six will not impress Number Seven, who will be suspicious of Number Six's polished and perfected image. In fact, it is unlikely that these two will find themselves at the same function.

If Number Six and Number Seven do find themselves attracted to each other and decide to become romantically involved, then they will probably be surprised at how well they get on. Number Seven is a very romantic individual, and Number Six will be flattered by his or her attentions and feel more confident about expressing his or her own emotions. Number Six will feel supported and loved by Number Seven but should remember to be attentive in return.

Problems will only arise if Number Seven feels unappreciated by Number Six and becomes insecure. Number Seven is able to express unhappiness in an emotional way and Number Six will not be able to cope with the resulting disharmony. Number Six should reassure Number Seven of his or her love on a regular basis and not just on birthdays, etc.

Once Number Six and Number Seven have worked through their initial difficulties they will be happy together. They will share an affectionate and loving relationship.

Birth Date Personality Number Six and Birth Date Personality Number Eight

Work
Number Six and Number Eight have the potential to form a very successful working partnership. Both are trustworthy and respected individuals who together will probably earn a reputation for producing good quality work.

Number Six's lack of ambition is compensated for by Number Eight's will to succeed. Number Eight is more able to cope with responsibility and everyday practicalities than Number Six. Number Six will be able to enhance the work of Number Eight by presenting it in its best light and knowing how to create the right image. Number Eight's stubbornness will be balanced by Number Six's ability to compromise and negotiate.

Number Six and Number Eight will respect and like each other and will gain a great deal from the experience of working together. It is unlikely that they will experience difficulties in working together as they will both be happy with their respective roles.

Romance
Number Eight will be attracted to Number Six because of his or her ability to project the right image and to stand out from the crowd. Number Six will be impressed by Number Eight's confidence and strength of character. This initial attraction may well lead to a relationship developing between Number Six and Number Eight.

The main difficulty in a relationship between Number Six and Number Eight is likely to be that neither individual will be willing to make the first move in terms of expressing emotions. Number Six is afraid of rejection and finds it difficult to express feelings, especially if he or she is uncertain whether those feelings will be reciprocated. Number Eight is cautious too. He or she generally waits for his or her partner to initiate any form of emotional dialogue. There is a danger that both individuals may decide that the other is not interested and that the relationship is not going to develop. Number Six and Number Eight should both try to be brave about declaring their feelings and should seriously consider making the first move if they do feel that they would like to become more involved.

If Number Six and Number Eight do find a way of communicating their feelings to each other and making a commitment, they will find that they enjoy a happy and loving relationship together. Number Six will be understanding of Number Eight, and Number Eight will be loving and attentive to Number Six. This is a relationship that should stand the test of time once the initial difficulties of communication have been worked through

Birth Date Personality Number Six and Birth Date Personality Number Nine

Work

Number Six and Number Nine will enjoy working together and will form a successful team. Number Six and Number Nine will find that their respective skills and talents complement each other well.

Number Six will find Number Nine's vision and energy inspirational and will feel motivated. Number Nine will recognize that Number Six's ability to promote and present are invaluable and will allow Number Six every opportunity to implement his or her skills. Number Six's negotiating and compromising skills will prove invaluable as a foil to Number Nine's tendency to be confrontational. Number Six and Number Nine will have distinct roles in their working relationship and they will both be happy with this.

Problems may arise if Number Nine insists on moving at a hectic pace and implements changes on a regular basis. Number Six needs harmony and balance and takes time to adapt to new introductions. Number Nine should be careful not to leave Number Six behind as Number Six may feel threatened and become insecure. If Number Six is unhappy, his or her work will suffer and he or she will probably think about looking for new employment. Number Nine should also be careful not to be confrontational with Number Six, who will not tolerate conflict.

If Number Nine and Number Six are both happy and move at the same pace they will enjoy a productive and enjoyable working relationship. As long as problems are avoided, Number Six and Number Nine could well go far together.

Romance
Number Six and Number Nine are both very attractive individuals who will be drawn to each other when they meet. Once they get to know each other, Number Six and Number Nine will be delighted to find that, for once, they have met someone who lives up to their expectations.

Number Six and Number Nine will enjoy a near-perfect relationship. Together they will find intensity and passion. Number Nine will be very demonstrative and romantic towards Number Six and will give him or her no reason to doubt the security of the relationship. In this relationship even Number Six, who can find expressing emotions difficult, will be completely at ease with vocal declarations and will be able to express love and devotion with confidence. Number Six and Number Nine will live together in almost dreamlike harmony, and it is most unlikely that they will experience any problems with each other.

The problems that this couple are likely to run into are generally with the realities of life outside their relationship. They may find it hard to accept the harsh realities of life, such as the necessity for money, food, heat, etc. Number Six and Number Nine need to recognize that although love will bring them much happiness it will not clothe and feed them and that at some point reality will have to enter their lives.

A relationship between Number Six and Number Nine will generally be extremely happy and long-lasting. They are very well suited to each other.

Birth Date Personality Number Seven and Birth Date Personality Number One *see* page 64

Birth Date Personality Number Seven and Birth Date Personality Number Two *see* page 81

Birth Date Personality Number Seven and Birth Date Personality Number Three *see* page 95

Birth Date Personality Number Seven and Birth Date Personality Number Seven

Work

Two Number Sevens working together will not find that their lives are dramatically affected by the experience but they will both be content. Neither individual is ambitious or has an interest in material wealth. Working together is not likely to increase either individual's personal motivation.

Both Number Sevens will, however, be hard-working and they will be valuable employees who can be counted on to get the job done. Each Number Seven will appreciate the other's hard work and honesty, and they will respect and admire each other. Both individuals will not tolerate dishonesty, and if one challenges a colleague's work practice on the grounds of dishonesty the other will be happy to provide full support.

Two Number Sevens will enjoy working together and will probably become good friends. They will understand each other's tendency to be vague and dreamy but will realize that this is because work is not of prime importance to them both. It will be a happy and enjoyable working relationship for both individuals but not one that will produce impressive results.

Romance

Two Number Sevens who are attracted to each other will soon find that the relationship will develop at a rapid pace. They will sweep each other off their feet and both will fall head over heels in love.

A relationship between two Number Sevens is likely to be a blissful affair, with both individuals feeling completely loved and secure. Two Number Sevens will fully understand each other's needs and desires and will have no difficulty in making each other happy. They will enjoy the opportunity to share their interest in literature and will discuss their favourite books for hours on end. Two Number Sevens romantically involved with each other will probably find that they spend much of their time talking to each other—a pastime of which neither will tire.

The only problem likely to arise for two Number Sevens is coping with reality. Neither will feel confident in dealing with household budgets or paying bills on time. There is a possibility that this couple could run into financial difficulties if they do not deal with financial issues as they arise. Both individuals have a tendency to put off unpleasant tasks. It is a good idea for two Number Sevens to share responsibility equally and tackle tasks together.

Two Number Sevens will enjoy a happy relationship together. It is a relationship that it is likely to last for a long time.

Birth Date Personality Number Seven and Birth Date Personality Number Eight

Work

Number Seven and Number Eight will enjoy a successful and productive working relationship together. Number Seven and Number Eight will find that their respective skills and talents will combine well together.

Number Eight will provide ambition and drive for success, which Number Seven lacks. Number Eight will be happy to take on responsibilities and make decisions. Number Eight enjoys feeling in control and Number Seven is happy to work without the added pressure of responsibility. Both Number Seven and Number Eight are hardworking individuals, and they will respect and admire each other's abilities. Number Seven will feel confident that Number Eight is an honest individual beside whom he or she feels that he or she can work in confidence. Number Eight will feel that Number Seven has more potential than he or she realizes and try to allow opportunities for Number Seven to develop new skills.

Number Eight should not try to dominate Number Seven. It is important that Number Seven feels that he or she is respected as an individual and that he or she is given space in which to work without being watched over. If Number Eight interferes too much in Number Seven's work, Number Seven may become resentful and feel less inclined to put in hard work.

Generally Number Seven and Number Eight will work well together and both will probably find it a rewarding experience.

Romance

There will be no dramatic first encounter for Number Seven and Number Eight. An attraction between these two is more likely to develop over a period of time in which they get to know each other.

If a romance does develop between Number Seven and Number Eight, the initial stages of the relationship will progress quite quickly. This will be unusual for Number Eight, who is generally quite reserved and cautious about making any sort of commitment, but Number Seven's ability to fall head over heels in love at the drop of a hat will ensure that commitment is discussed at an early stage. This will suit both individuals initially.

Problems may arise if Number Eight feels too confident of Number Seven's love and takes the relationship for granted. Number Eight may feel so sure of Number Seven's devotion that he or she feels that he or she can spend less time with his or her partner and more time at work advancing his or her career. Number Seven needs love and support and may become insecure and resentful if he or she feels that Number Eight is neglecting him or her. Number Seven should not be too demanding of Number Eight and should appreciate that his or her career is very important to him or her. There could be difficulties in communication generally between Number Seven and Number Eight. Number Seven will not really understand Number Eight's ambitions, and Number Eight may find Number Seven too emotionally demanding and a bit vague and unmotivated. Number Seven may feel that Number Eight is too domineering and may feel that his or her independence is being threatened.

Number Seven and Number Eight have quite a few problems that they will need to work through in order for this relationship to succeed. If Number Seven and Number Eight do manage to overcome their differences then they will be happy together.

Birth Date Personality Number Seven and Birth Date Personality Number Nine

Work

Number Seven and Number Nine will enjoy the experience of working together and will find that they work well together. Number Seven and Number Nine have quite different approaches to work but their differences complement each other.

Number Nine's vision and ambition will be a source of inspiration for Number Seven, who does not usually feel motivated by work. Number Nine will be happy to take on the majority of responsibility and absorb the associated stress. Number Nine thrives on working under pressure, and Number Seven likes a stress-free working environment. Number Nine will be able to enjoy creating a frenzy of activity for himself or herself whilst allowing Number Seven to work away in peace. Number Nine will appreciate Number Seven's hard work and will respect his or her need for independence.

Number Nine and Number Seven will respect and admire each other and they will both benefit from the experience of working together. In their working relationship Number Seven and Number Nine will experience few difficulties and will get on well together.

Romance

Number Seven and Number Nine are both very romantic individuals and will find themselves drawn to each other when they first meet. An attraction between Number Seven and Number Nine will develop quickly into a more serious relationship. Both individuals are likely to fall head over heels in love after a short time.

If Number Seven and Number Nine do find themselves

involved in a romantic relationship with each other, they will be very happy together. They will enjoy a passionate and intense relationship. They will find themselves fully absorbed by one another. There is a danger that Number Seven and Number Nine will be so obsessed by each other that they will neglect everyone and everything else. The end result of this could be losing touch with reality all together. Number Seven and Number Nine will have little interest in doing anything other than spending time with each other.

Number Seven and Number Nine will enjoy a harmonious relationship in which they both feel appreciated and loved. Number Nine, who has a tendency to be jealous, will have no reason to doubt Number Seven's commitment to the relationship, and Number Seven will not feel insecure because he or she will be so confident of Number Nine's love. Number Seven and Number Nine are not likely to part once they have found each other.

Birth Date Personality Number Eight and Birth Date Personality Number One *see* **page 67**

Birth Date Personality Number Eight and Birth Date Personality Number Two *see* **page 83**

Birth Date Personality Number Eight and Birth Date Personality Number Three *see* **page 97**

Birth Date Personality Number Eight and Birth Date Personality Number Four *see* **page 112**

Birth Date Personality Number Eight and Birth Date Personality Number Five *see* **page 123**

Birth Date Personality Number Eight and Birth Date Personality Number Six *see* **page 131**

Birth Date Personality Number Eight and Birth Date Personality Number Seven *see* **page 138**

Birth Date Personality Number Eight and Birth Date Personality Number Eight

Work

Two Number Eights working together have the potential to achieve great success. However, in order to do this, both individuals will have to put effort into establishing a strong working relationship.

Two Number Eights will both be very confident and strong-willed individuals who are used to getting their own way. They may find that working with each other is frustrating if they do not allow each other space and independence. If two Number Eights try to work together too closely they will find that they will waste important time and energy locked in trying to dominate each other. Both individuals are uncompromising and stubborn, and any dispute between them is unlikely to be resolved. Two Number Eights will find the experience of working together far more rewarding if they acknowledge each other's talents and skills and respect each other's work practices. Two Number Eights should work together, not in opposition, and should establish clearly defined roles for each individual so that they can both work independently.

Once two Number Eights are established in their respective roles and are happy working together, they will begin to achieve a great deal together. The combined confidence and abilities of two Number Eights will be a powerful force, and they will go far. Over time, two Number Eights will begin to admire and respect each other and may even become close friends.

Romance
Two Number Eights are likely to be attracted to each other's confidence and contentment. They will admire each other, and from respect there is a chance that romance may blossom.

The main problem for two Number Eights romantically involved with each other is that neither individual will be willing to make the first move in terms of declaring any feelings about the relationship. Both individuals prefer to wait for their partner to take the initiative in terms of displaying emotions. There is a danger that the relationship between two Number Eights will never develop if they are both unwilling to broach the subject of commitment. If the relationship does not develop, both Number Eights may decide that the relationship is going nowhere and call it off. Both Number Eights need to be more confident and assertive in expressing their emotions if they do not want to miss out on a potentially successful relationship.

If two Number Eights do make a commitment to each other, they will find that they enjoy a harmonious and pleasant relationship with each other. It will not be a passionate or particularly romantic relationship, but both individuals will feel supported and loved within it. Both Number Eights will have a tendency to spend the majority of their time at work or in pursuit of career success. In relationships with other people, this can cause problems, but two Number Eights will fully understand each other's ambitions and need to succeed.

Once two Number Eights open up and admit their true feelings for each other, they will find that they are kindred spirits and will be happy to make a commitment to each other. Once a relationship between two Number Eights has been established, they will stay together for a long time because they feel happy and secure in the relationship.

Birth Date Personality Number Eight and Birth Date Personality Number Nine

Work
Number Eight and Number Nine will find working together

challenging but rewarding. Number Eight and Number Nine are similar characters in many ways, but they do have significant differences in their approach to work.

Number Eight and Number Nine are both confident and determined individuals. Number Nine has more vision than Number Eight and is more creative. Number Eight is more committed and practical than Number Nine. Number Eight is better at delegating work and negotiating with other colleagues than Number Nine. Both individuals have great organizational skills and are able to create effective work structures. Both individuals are happy to take on responsibility and make decisions. Between them Number Eight and Number Nine possess all the skills and talents necessary for success and if they work together they will probably go far.

Problems arise in the working relationship between Number Eight and Number Nine if they find themselves trying to dominate or change each other. Both individuals have very strong personalities, and neither is likely to back down from a confrontation. Number Eight and Number Nine need to acknowledge their similarities and differences and respect each other. Number Nine and Number Eight both need independence in their working environment and they should avoid working together too closely.

If Number Eight and Number Nine do manage to resolve their differences, they will find that working together is a rewarding experience. Both have a great deal that they can learn from each other.

Romance

Number Eight and Number Nine will probably find that there is an instant attraction between them when they meet. Number Eight will be captivated by Number Nine's energy and vitality, and Number Nine will find Number Eight's confidence and strength of character irresistible.

A relationship between Number Eight and Number Nine will develop quite quickly. Number Eight prefers to wait for his or her partner to take the initiative in terms of voicing feelings and discussing commitment. Number Eight will be happy to discover that Number Nine has no difficulty in taking the lead in this area, and Number Nine will gladly declare undying love for Number Eight and suggest that they make a commitment to one another.

Number Eight and Number Nine will generally find that they enjoy a harmonious relationship together. Number Eight has a tendency to take relationships for granted and to neglect his or her partner in favour of spending more time on his or her career. Number Nine will not stand for this and will demand Number Eight's full attention. In a relationship with Number Nine, Number Eight will be happy to devote time to the relationship and will be less preoccupied with work.

Number Eight and Number Nine are well suited in terms of romance. They will find that, if they are committed to each other, their life together will be a happy one.

Birth Date Personality Number Nine and Birth Date Personality Number One *see* page 69

Birth Date Personality Number Nine and Birth Date Personality Number Two *see* page 85

Birth Date Personality Number Nine and Birth Date Personality Number Three *see* page 99

Birth Date Personality Number Nine and Birth Date Personality Number Four *see* page 114

Birth Date Personality Number Nine and Birth Date Personality Number Five *see* page 125

Birth Date Personality Number Nine and Birth Date Personality Number Six *see* page 133

Birth Date Personality Number Nine and Birth Date Personality Number Seven *see* page 140

Birth Date Personality Number Nine and Birth Date Personality Number Eight *see* page 145

Birth Date Personality Number Nine and Birth Date Personality Number Nine

Work

Two Number Nines will enjoy the experience of working together. If they are working together on a project that interests them they will work well together and achieve great results.

Two Number Nines will find each other enthusiastic and energetic and will instantly hit it off. They will enjoy discussing their ideas and visions with each other and will find each other to be a source of further inspiration. Both individuals enjoy working under pressure, and they will be happy to join forces to work hard to meet deadlines. Both Number Nines will be organized and efficient in their work, and they are unlikely to fail to meet any deadline.

Two Number Nines will be very similar in their approach to their work, and in some areas they will find difficulties arising. Both individuals are more concerned with visions for the future and grand plans than with the finer details and practicalities. Both have a tendency to tire of a project before it is completed and lose interest in the finished product. Two Number Nines working together should ensure that another colleague is willing to take on the responsibility of overseeing the completion of projects or they may find that they earn themselves a reputation for slapdash work. Number Nines have no fear of making bold decisions, and two Number Nines together should be wary of being too bold to the point of carelessness.

Two Number Nines will enjoy each other's company in the working environment and will even enjoy the regular confrontations that will occur between them. Number Nines are forceful characters who frequently run into conflict. Two Number Nines will understand that these disputes are unimportant and may even feel that they add to the excitement of working together.

Romance

There is little doubt that two Number Nines will be instantly attracted to each other when they first meet. They will be fascinated by each other's energy and vitality and will want to get to know each other better.

A relationship between two Number Nines will develop very quickly, and they will soon find themselves committed to each other. Two Number Nines will enjoy a passionate and romantic relationship together. They will be able to understand each other completely and fulfil each other's needs. Two Number Nines will enjoy each other's company and spend all their free time together.

Number Nines are very emotional characters, and two Number Nines involved in a romantic relationship will find that, although blissfully happy together, they will have many dramatic arguments. Two Number Nines will thrive on a cycle of screaming arguments followed by passionate reunions. Both individuals will enjoy the drama and excitement and fully accept arguing as an important aspect of their relationship.

Two Number Nines will understand each other fully and will be extremely happy together. A relationship between these two individuals is likely to last for a very long time.

Birth Chart

Although your birth date number is the most significant number in your life, it does not have sole influence over your personality. Your birth date number is calculated using the series of numbers that formulate your date of birth. Each number within this series has an influence on your relationship with your birth date number. Two people who share the same birth date number may have very different birth charts and therefore different characteristics.

To find out more about yourself from your birth chart use the simple process shown below.

For reference, look at the complete birth chart that indicates the way in which numbers are recorded in a birth chart (figure 1).

3	6	9
2	5	8
1	4	7

Step 1: Write out your date of birth in numerical form.
e.g. 27th August 1965, 27.08.1965

Step 2 : Discard any zeros from the series of numbers.
e.g. 27.8.1965
Step 3: Record the numbers in the birth chart.
e.g. (figure 2)

There is a blank grid for you to record your birth chart (figure 3).

It is important to record a number every time it appears, even if you have four or more of one number.

Number Lines

The next step is to study your completed Birth Chart to look for complete and missing number lines, diagonally, vertically and horizontally. These lines are known as the Arrows of Pythagoras and are associated with particular personality traits. If we look at our example (figure 2) we can see that there is a complete number line, 1-5-9 which is The Line of Determination.

The number lines and their characteristics are listed below.

1-5-9 The Line of Determination (figure 4)

The presence of this complete number line in a birth chart indicates resoluteness, persistence, dedication, strong will, tenacity, firmness of purpose, conviction, fortitude and stamina.

1-5-9 missing The Line of Resignation (figure 5)

The lack of any numbers present in this line indicates lack of motivation, submission, lack of enthusiasm, unwillingness, lack of determination and lack of originality.

3-5-7 The Line of Compassion (figure 6)

The presence of this line in a birth chart indicates sympathy, humanity, kindness, understanding, benevolence and intuition.

153

3-5-7 missing The Line of Scepticism (figure 7)

The lack of any numbers present in this line indicates doubtfulness, lack of trust, suspicion, disbelief, incredulity and cynicism.

3-6-9 Line of the Intellect (figure 8)

The presence of this line in a birth chart indicates intelligence, creative thought, the ability to solve problems and mental agility.

3-6-9 missing The Line of Eccentricity (figure 9)

The lack of any numbers present in this line indicates unconventional thought, nonconformity, lack of logic and individuality.

2-5-8 The Line of Emotion (figure 10)

The presence of this line in a birth chart indicates sensitivity, spirituality, balance, harmony, calm and love.

2-5-8 missing The Line of Sensitivity (figure 11)

The lack of any numbers in this line indicates, shyness, a sense of inferiority, and a tendency to be oversensitive and introverted.

1-4-7 The Line of Physicality (figure 12)

The presence of this line in a birth chart indicates good health, manual dexterity, action, skill, practicality and ability.

1-4-7 missing The Line of Illusion (figure 13)

The lack of any numbers present in this line indicates insecurity, weakness, uncertainty, a tendency to be accident-prone, a lack of practicality and a non-materialistic approach to life.

1-2-3 The Line of the Planner (figure 14)

The presence of this line in a birth chart indicates consideration, neatness, administrative skills, organisational abilities and leadership qualities.

1-2-3 missing The Line of Confusion (figure 15)

The lack of any numbers present in this line indicates disorder, chaos, a lack of balance, muddle and disorganisation.

4-5-6 The Line of Will (figure 16)

The presence of this line in a birth chart indicates ambition, determination, single-mindedness, clarity of purpose and direction.

4-5-6 missing The Line of Frustration (figure 17)

The lack of any numbers present in this line indicates a lack of fulfilment, dissatisfaction, disappointment, discontent, resentment and a lack of success.

7-8-9 The Line of Action (figure 18)

The presence of this line in a birth chart indicates enthusiasm, zeal, energy, vitality, power, activity and decisiveness.

7-8-9 missing The Line of Inertia (figure 19)

The lack of any numbers present in this line indicates inactivity, stagnation, passivity, listlessness, idleness and contemplation.

Further information about your character can be gained by studying how frequently numbers appear in your chart.

One (birth chart figures 20-24)

one x one (figure 20)

People who have one one in their birth chart may find that they have difficulty in expressing their emotions in their personal lives. They may find that they are confident in expressing themselves in non-personal matters. Other people can view their lack of emotion as an indication that they are cold and uncaring people.

two x one (figure 21)

People who have two ones in their birth chart will experience no difficulty at all in expressing themselves. These people tend to have well-balanced approaches to life.

three x one (figure 22)

People who have three ones in their birth chart are usually blessed with wonderful communication skills. They are confident in their own abilities but can at times be viewed as arrogant.

four or more x one (figure 23)

People with four or more ones in their birth chart may find life frustrating because they set themselves unattainable goals.

one missing (figure 24)

People who have no ones in their birth chart tend to lack determination, confidence and assertiveness.

Two (birth chart figures 25-29)

one x two (figure 25)

People who have one two in their birth chart are generally sensitive individuals who have no enthusiasm for competition. They are easily hurt by the criticism of others.

two x two (figure 26)

People who have two twos in their birth chart tend to be very perceptive people who are able to accurately assess others.

three x two (figure 27)

222		

People who have three twos in their birth chart are very sensitive individuals. They tend to put up emotional barriers and may appear to be uncaring but this is the opposite of the truth.

four or more x two (figure 28)

22 22+		

People who have four or more twos in their birth chart have a tendency to overreact. They are often highly strung individuals who are prone to flashes of ill-temper.

two missing (figure 29)

People who have no twos in their birth chart tend to be uncooperative, inconsiderate and unappreciative of other people.

Three (birth chart figures 30-34)

one x three (figure 30)

3		

People who have one three in their birth chart are creative and intelligent, imaginative and are stimulating company.

two x three (figure 31)

33		

People who have two number threes in their birth chart tend to have very vivid imaginations and a tendency to daydream.

three x three (figure 32)

333		

People with three threes in their birth chart tend to be absorbed in their own thoughts. These people may lose contact with family and friends if they become too reclusive.

four or more x three (figure 33)

People with four or more threes in their birth chart may find that their mental activity is hard to control and may be prone to anxiety and confusion.

three missing (figure 34)

People who have no threes in their birth chart tend to lack imagination and creativity.

Four (birth chart figures 35-39)

one x four (figure 35)

People with one four in their birth chart are practical and

organised. They are often good with their hands. They enjoy the satisfaction of seeing a finished product.

two x four (figure 36)

People who have two fours in their birth chart are neat and tidy and very good with their hands. They are hard working people and put a great deal of effort into their careers.

three x four (figure 37)

People with three fours in their birth chart are very hard working individuals. They can become preoccupied with their careers and sometimes neglect other aspects of their lives.

four or more x four (figure 38)

People with four or more fours in their birth chart are often workaholics who are very talented and able. These people should allow themselves time to relax and enjoy themselves.

four missing (figure 39)

People with no fours in their birth chart tend to dislike practicalities and are often careless and lacking in determination.

Five (birth chart figures 40-44)

one x five (figure 40)

People with one five in their birth chart are determined individuals who have strong characters. They have the ability to motivate other people and are strong-willed. They have a need for freedom and independence.

two x five (figure 41)

	55	

People with two fives in their birth chart are determined but may have a tendency to be overly confident.

three x five (figure 42)

	555	

People with three fives in their birth chart are self-assured and completely determined. There is a danger that if they are too focused on themselves they will disregard the needs of others.

four or more x five (figure 43)

	55 55	

People with four or more fives in their birth chart tend to enjoy living life in the fast lane. They have a tendency to take risks and thrive on drama and excitement.

five missing (figure 44)

People who have no fives in their birth chart tend to lack determination and motivation.

Six (birth chart figures 45-49)

one x six (figure 45)

People with one six in their birth chart are home-lovers who need a harmonious and relaxed environment in which to live.

two x six (figure 46)

People with two sixes in their birth chart tend to regard their home as being centrally important to their lives. They have a tendency to be very protective of their home and dislike leaving it.

three x six (figure 47)

<table>
<tr><td></td><td>6
66</td><td></td></tr>
<tr><td></td><td></td><td></td></tr>
<tr><td></td><td></td><td></td></tr>
</table>

People who have three sixes in their birth chart are protective of their home and their loved ones and are prone to becoming anxious over minor matters.

four or more x six (figure 48)

<table>
<tr><td></td><td>66
+
66</td><td></td></tr>
<tr><td></td><td></td><td></td></tr>
<tr><td></td><td></td><td></td></tr>
</table>

People with four or more sixes in their birth chart tend to be very creative individuals but they may find difficulties in controlling their emotions.

six missing (figure 49)

People who have no sixes in their birth chart tend to have little regard for their home environment.

Seven (birth chart figures 50-54)

one x seven (figure 50)

People with one seven in their birth chart dislike injustice. They want to learn about truth by themselves.

two x seven (figure 51)

People with two sevens in their birth chart have a real interest in the meaning of life. They are self-reliant individuals.

three x seven (figure 52)

People who have three sevens in their birth chart tend to be wise and mature. To gain their knowledge and understanding they will have faced many difficult situations in their lives.

four or more x seven (figure 53)

People with four or more sevens are strong-willed individuals who are willing to face adversity in their pursuit of true understanding.

seven missing (figure 54)

People who have no seven in their birth chart have a need for the company of others. They do not tend to like their own company and have no interest in spiritual or metaphysical matters.

Eight (birth chart figures 55–59)

one x eight (figure 55)

People who have one eight in their birth chart tend to have the ability to assess the abilities of others. They are good at organising and pay attention to detail.

two x eight (figure 56)

People who have two eights in their birth chart tend to be extremely efficient and capable individuals. Their ability to assess situations can sometimes strike others as intimidating.

three x eight (figure 57)

People who have three eights in their birth chart will often find that they achieve career success late in life once they have experimented with the various options open to them.

four or more x eight (figure 58)

People with four or more eights in their birth chart may find that they are very successful in their chosen careers. They should guard against becoming too fixated on material wealth.

eight missing (figure 59)

People who have no eight in their birth chart lack organisational abilities and have a tendency to careless with money.

Nine (see birth chart figures 60–64)

one x nine (figure 60)

People with one nine in their birth charts are often idealists who have a desire to achieve perfection in their lives.

two x nine (figure 61)

People who have two nines in their birth chart are creative and emotional individuals who feel the need to make a difference. These people set themselves unachievable goals which can lead to frustration and disappointment.

three x nine (figure 62)

People with three nines in their birth chart frequently feel the need to create perfection in their lives. They can become single-minded in their pursuit of utopia and are in danger of becoming cut off from reality.

four or more x nine (figure 63)

People who have four or more nines in their birth chart often have very high expectations of themselves and others and can find life frustrating and disappointing.

nine missing (figure 64)

People who have no nine in their birth chart are not primarily concerned with human welfare and often lack the ability to view things in broad terms.

The Numerology of Names

As we have seen in the previous section, numerologists believe that a great deal can be interpreted about your personality and life by analysing your birth date. It has been stated that your birth date holds the most significant information about you in terms of numerology.

In this section we will discover that more information can be learned about you and your motivation by studying your name. Name numbers are less prominent than your birth date number and are considered by some numerologists to have secondary significance. This is because you are not tied to your name in the same way that you are to your birth date. It is possible to change your name. It is not possible to alter your date of birth.

Your name affects how other people react to you. On simply hearing a name people make assumptions about the person that owns it before they even meet. This is because your name is a word, and words form the basis of communication in our society. Every word means something to somebody. Your name is no exception.

Your name is a personal symbol that is inseparable from

you. It has been chosen for you and you will react to it in your own individual way.

The name that you choose to work with for purposes of numerology is entirely up to you. Some numerologists insist that you must use the full name that is on your birth certificate as they believe that this is the true name. Other numerologists argue that the name most commonly used should be the one that is analysed. The choice is yours, but it is probably best to use the name that you identify most strongly with.

If you are known by more than one name and are unsure which one to analyse, try working with both names and see which is the one that you think gives you most insight into yourself. It could be that you are a mixture of the two names and do not really truly belong to either one.

If you have changed your name, it is interesting to analyse the name you are known by now and compare it with the name you used to be known by. This often reveals a process of change and development.

Your first name affects your personal life and has the strongest influence on your personality. Your surname indicates the traits and characteristics that you have inherited and has less effect on your personality. If you are always known by your surname it will have greater significance and should be treated as a first name. Your full name provides the complete picture of you and how other people view you.

There are three numerical aspects of your name that can be

analysed: the vowel number, the consonant number and the full name number.

To analyse the name, it is first necessary to break down the alphabet so that every letter has a number associated with it. This is done by the process of fadic addition. A = 1 because it is the first number in the alphabet, M = 4 because M is the thirteenth number in the alphabet and 1 + 3 = 4 and Z = 8 because Z is the twenty-sixth number in the alphabet and 2 + 6 = 8, and so on.

The complete alphabet and the numbers associated with each letter are recorded in the chart below:

1	2	3	4	5	6	7	8	9
A	B	C	D	E	F	G	H	I
J	K	L	M	N	O	P	Q	R
S	T	U	V	W	X	Y	Z	

The Vowel Number

The vowel number is also known as the motivation number, the ambition number, the heart's desire number and other names. We shall simply refer to it as the vowel number.

In terms of the numerology of names, the vowel number is second only in importance to the whole name number. The vowel number indicates your ambitions and desires. From analysing the make-up of your name, it is possible to identify areas of conflict in your life that arise from incompatible numbers. Your vowel number, for example, may not be the same as your birth date number, and so your vowel number dictates that you have an ambition that your birth date number dictates will not be achieved.

The vowels are A, E, I, O and U. If you have no vowels in your name but do have a Y, the Y can be interpreted as a vowel. If you have vowels and a Y in your name, you can analyse your name twice, once using the Y as a vowel and once using it as a consonant.

The numbers that represent each vowel are listed below.

A = 1   E = 5   I = 9   O = 6   U = 3   Y = 7

To find your vowel number follow the steps listed below.

Step 1: Write out the name that you have chosen to work with.

Example: CAROLINE MACDONALD

Step 2: Place the number for each vowel above the appropriate letter.

Example:

```
  1   6   9 5   1     6   1
CAROLINE MACDONALD
```

Step 3: Add all the numbers together.

Example: $1 + 6 + 9 + 5 + 1 + 6 + 1 = 29$

Step 4: Using the process of fadic addition (continuing to add the numbers together until a single digit number remains) reduce this figure to a number between 1 and 9.

Example: $2 + 9 = 11 > 1 + 1 = 2$

In our example the vowel number for Caroline Macdonald is 2.

Vowel Number One

People with vowel number one want to take charge and to be in control. Freedom and independence are very important to people with vowel number one. They do not like to be dictated to by others. They need to be in charge of their own lives. They are generally optimistic people who have a great deal of inner strength. They are often a source of inspiration to other people.

People with vowel number one are determined individuals who occasionally overlook the wants and needs of others in the pursuit of their own goals.

Vowel Number Two

People with vowel number two do not have any desire to take the lead or be in control. They want to follow others. They want balance and harmony in their lives. They achieve this through negotiation and compromise, at which they are extremely skilled. They need to be able to get on with other people. They want to avoid conflict and competition in their lives.

People with vowel number two are easy-going individuals who are well liked but occasionally taken advantage.

Vowel Number Three

People with vowel number three want life to be enjoyable. They seek to bring pleasure into their own and other people's lives. They are cheerful and optimistic people,

179

and they are usually lively conversationalists and entertaining company. They need to feel popular and want people to like them. They are hard-working but know when to stop and how to enjoy themselves in their spare time.

People with vowel number three are confident and outgoing and other people occasionally regard them as being full of themselves.

Vowel Number Four

People with vowel number four want orderly and conventional lives. They need organization in their lives and want 'a place for everything and everything in its place'. They are very practical and efficient individuals who work hard in pursuit of security and stability. They are dependable and reliable people who need to have a purpose in life.

People with vowel number four can overwork themselves and need to allow themselves time to relax.

Vowel Number Five

People with vowel number five want variety and change in their lives. They need to feel free and unrestricted to explore life and have adventures. They need to be able to expand their knowledge by having new experiences. They are adaptable and versatile people who enjoy the challenge of adjusting to a new environment. They need to travel to broaden their horizons.

People with vowel number five can become restless and

frustrated if they find that life does not move at a fast enough pace to meet their needs.

Vowel Number Six

People with vowel number six want peace and harmony in their lives. They have a strong sense of responsibility for the wellbeing of others. They need to believe that justice is being done and cannot abide injustice. They are very caring people and need the opportunity to give and receive love. They need to be able to create a home environment where they can feel safe and secure.

People with vowel number six can be overprotective and may become anxious and nervous.

Vowel Number Seven

People with vowel number seven need to be able to spend a great deal of time alone with their thoughts. They need a peaceful and private space in which they can contemplate life. They are very independent individuals and do not want to be told what to do by others. They are great thinkers and are often very perceptive. People with vowel number seven are more likely than most to have psychic powers. They have a love of natural beauty and need to spend time in natural surroundings, away from civilization.

People with vowel number seven may become frustrated and unhappy if they are not allowed to have enough personal space and freedom.

Vowel Number Eight
People with vowel number eight have a burning desire to succeed and are very ambitious individuals. They need to be self-reliant and independent. They do not want to feel at the mercy of anyone else. They are usually great organizers and are confident in their own abilities. They want to be in responsible positions and have no fear of making decisions.

People with vowel number eight may set themselves unachievable goals and become frustrated if they are not able to meet them.

Vowel Number Nine
People with vowel number nine want life to meet their ideals. They want the world to be a better place. They want everyone to be happy and at peace. They are compassionate and caring individuals who have romantic notions. They have a great love of life and want to live life to the full. They have a great fondness for their fellow humans and want to spend a great deal of their time talking and sharing thoughts.

People with vowel number nine tend to try to do too much at one time and can let themselves become exhausted.

Consonant Number
The consonant number is also known as the external image number, the impression number, the inner self number and other names. We shall simply refer to it as the con-

sonant number. The consonant number indicates how you present yourself in public. It gives you insight into how other people regard you. The consonant number does not reflect who you actually are but shows what other people think you are like. The consonant number is the least important of the numbers that are found by analysing your name but helps to build up a complete picture of you.

The consonants are all the letters in the alphabet that are not vowels. The numbers associated with each consonant are listed below:

B = 2   C = 3   D = 4   F = 6   G = 7   H = 8   J = 1
K = 2   L = 3   M = 4   N = 5   P = 7   Q = 8   R = 9
S = 1   T = 2   V = 4   W = 5   X = 6   Y = 7   Z = 8

To find your consonant number, simply follow the steps listed below:

Step 1: Write out the name that you have chosen to work with.

Example: CAROLINE MACDONALD

Step 2 :Place the appropriate number beneath each consonant in the name.

Example: CAROLINE MACDONALD
         3 9 3 5 4 34 5 34

Step 3: Add all the numbers together.

Example: 3 + 9 + 3 + 5 + 4 + 3 + 4 + 5 + 3 + 4 = 43

Step 4 : Using the process of fadic addition reduce this number to a single unit.

Example: $4 + 3 = 7$

In our example the name Caroline Macdonald has the consonant number 7.

Consonant Number One

People with consonant number one present a cool, calm and collected image. They appear to be unique individuals who stand out from the crowd. They send out signals of confidence and self-reliance saying that they do not want anyone's help. They project an air of being in control of every situation. They appear to be determined to face life alone and do not want to work closely with other people. They seem to be happy people who find it easy to make friends.

Consonant Number Two

People with consonant number two seem to want not to be noticed. They seem to make an effort to merge in with the background. They seem to be uncomfortable if they are the centre of attention. They appear to want to avoid conflict, and they project an image of being a diplomat and negotiator who seems to be able to find a compromise in any situation. They seem to be approachable and friendly and willing to listen. They seem to be warm and comforting people who are trustworthy and reliable.

Consonant Number Three

People with consonant number three appear to be the life

and soul of the party. They appear to be bright, enthusiastic and entertaining individuals. They seem to live life to the full and know how to enjoy themselves fully. They appear to thrive on the company of others and seem always to be willing to make new friends. They seem to be intelligent people who have the ability to make others laugh. They seem to need excitement in their lives and enjoy a hectic social life. They seem to be popular individuals and are often the first people to be invited to any social events.

Consonant Number Four

People with consonant number four appear to be practical and organized individuals who have no fear of hard work and responsibility. They seem to be trustworthy individuals who are 'as straight as they come'. They appear to be the type to play everything by the book and never bend the rules or leave anything to chance. They seem to be disciplined and in charge of their emotions. They appear to be confident of their own abilities and to know what they want from life. They appear to have a fondness for traditions and seem conservative in their approach to life. They seem to be admired for their honesty and hard work.

Consonant Number Five

People with consonant number five appear to be multi-talented individuals who can turn a hand to whatever takes their fancy. They seem to be adaptable individuals who have the ability to captivate an audience. They appear to be constantly on the move and looking for new challenges. They seem to be constantly in pursuit of new experiences and opportunities to broaden their horizons. They seem unpredictable and transient. They appear to need a great deal of independence and personal freedom, and seem not to want to become too involved with anyone.

Consonant Number Six

People with consonant number six appear to be responsible and nurturing individuals who are willing to offer support and protection to other people. They seem to be calm and balanced people who are content with their lives. They seem to be blessed with creative talents and appear to have the ability to make anywhere feel like home. People seem to be drawn to people with birth date number six and seek their advice and opinions. They seem to have near-perfect lives.

Consonant Number Seven

People with consonant number seven appear to be distant and mysterious. They seem to be absorbed in their own thoughts for much of the time and appear to be unapproachable. They seem to be secretive and unwilling to share their thoughts with others. It seems that they enjoy their own company and are not particularly interested in making new friends. They appear to be intelligent and perceptive people who are considered to be philosophical and observant. They appear to live their lives outwith the norms of society.

Consonant Number Eight
People with consonant number eight appear to be almost larger than life. They seem to be self-assured and completely confident. They seem to dominate the company that they are in. They appear to be strong characters who have a great deal of power that they know how to use. They have an air of success and project an image of being at ease with themselves and their surroundings. They seem to want to be regarded as a figure of authority and want to be in control. They seem to be respected for their ambition and abilities.

Consonant Number Nine
People with consonant number nine seem to be non-judgmental and open-minded individuals who are happy to accept everyone whom they meet as their equal. They appear to love everyone and have a great deal of compassion and tenderness towards their fellow human beings. They appear to have many creative talents and unique abilities. They seem to be determined to live their lives as they choose. They appear to be emotional and understanding individuals who enjoy the company of others and always have time to talk and listen. They seem to be popular and regarded as good friends.

Whole Name Number
The whole name number is also known as the expression number, the destiny number, the life mission number and

the character number. We shall simply call it the whole name number. The whole name number is the most important number that can be derived from your name. The whole name number indicates what you actually do and gives insight into your ability to interact with others. The whole name number is very important because you have the power to change it. By changing your name you can change your whole name number and so change what you do.

The whole name number is calculated by adding together all the numbers in your name. To do this we should again refer to the chart that shows which numbers correspond with the letters of the alphabet.

1	2	3	4	5	6	7	8	9
A	B	C	D	E	F	G	H	I
J	K	L	M	N	O	P	Q	R
S	T	U	V	W	X	Y	Z	

Simply follow the steps listed below:

Step 1: Write out the full name that you have chosen.

Example: CAROLINE MACDONALD

Step 2: Place the appropriate numbers above the vowels and below the consonants.

Example:

```
  1 6 9 5   1   6 1
CAROLINE MACDONALD
3 9 3 5   4 34 5   34
```

Step 3: There are two ways to do this next step.

(1) Add together all the vowel numbers. Add together all the consonant numbers. Then add both totals together.
Example:
$1 + 6 + 9 + 5 + 1 + 6 + 1 = 29$
$3 + 9 + 3 + 5 + 4 + 3 + 4 + 5 + 3 + 4 = 43$
$29 + 43 = 72$
(2) Add all the numbers together.
Example: $1 + 6 + 9 + 5 + 1 + 6 + 1 + 3 + 9 + 3 + 5 + 4 + 3 + 4 + 5 + 3 + 4 = 72$
The end result should be the same no matter which method you use.
Step 4: Now use the process of fadic addition to reduce this number to a single unit.
Example: $7 + 2 = 9$
In our example the whole name number is 9.

Whole Name Number One—The Leader
People with the whole name number one are assertive and confident in their interaction with other people. They are happy to take on the role of leader and are comfortable with responsibility and making decisions. They are open-minded and willing to experiment with new experiences. They are bold in their actions and are often the first to take a step in a new direction. They believe in themselves and in their ability to succeed.

People with the whole name number one can be self-centred and may disregard the desires and needs of others. They can be too ambitious and become impatient in waiting for success.

Whole Name Number Two—The Mediator
People with the whole name number two are friendly and approachable in their interaction with other people. They are tactful and diplomatic individuals who are able to cooperate well with other people. They have valuable negotiating skills and are able to find ways in which to achieve compromise. They enjoy peaceful surroundings and often have an appreciation of the arts. They are sympathetic towards others and appreciate the support of others in return.

People with the whole name number two can be indecisive. They also are sometimes guilty of dishonesty. In their attempts to keep the peace they will sometimes fail to tell the truth.

Whole Name Number Three—The Optimist
People with the whole name number three are lively and entertaining in their interaction with other people. They are great communicators and often have a brilliant command of language. They are witty and intelligent people who make full use of their talents. They are fun-loving individuals who love to socialize. They are often blessed with creative talents that they need to be able to utilise.

People with whole name number three can lack organization in their lives and they may find that they try to do too many things at any one time.

Whole Name Number Four—The Builder

People with the whole name number four are down to earth and practical in their interaction with other people. They are organized and efficient individuals who work hard to achieve their ambitions. They are respected and admired by other people because of their commitment and determination. They are thoughtful people who never rush into situations without considering the consequences. They have a very logical approach to life and know what they want to achieve. They are conservative with a fondness for tradition.

People with the whole name number four can work too hard and push themselves too far. They can also be narrow-minded and find it hard to accept people different from themselves.

Whole Name Number Five—The Chameleon

People with the whole name number five are open and adaptable in their interaction with other people. They have a versatile approach to life and are happy to embrace change. They do not like to have restrictions imposed upon them and have a strong need for personal freedom and independence. They are interested in discovering about the various theories relating to the purpose of life and are always receptive to new input from other people. They have an optimistic approach to life and view every new experience as an opportunity to learn something new.

People with the whole name number five may find that

they are constantly on the move and lose touch with friends and family. They may find that some people are distrustful of their unconventional approach to life.

Whole Name Number Six—Home Lover

People with the whole name number six are kind and caring in their interaction with other people. They are balanced and calm individuals who enjoy harmonious surroundings. They are responsible people who take on the role of protecting others. They are always willing to offer a helping hand to anyone in need. They create warm and comfortable home environments, which are very important to them and which they will defend strongly.

People with the whole name number six can sometimes be patronizing to other people and offer help where it is not wanted.

Whole Name Number Seven—The Thinker

People with the whole name number seven do not feel bound by the conventions of society and will interact with other people as they see fit at any given time. They are self-reliant and independent individuals who choose to learn about life for themselves. They do not want to learn from the experiences of others or to listen to other people's advice. They enjoy their own company and need time and space to be alone with their thoughts.

People with the whole name number seven may become lost in their own thoughts and eventually lose touch with reality. They are not confident in their decision making and sometimes opportunities will pass them by while they consider their options.

Whole Name Number Eight—The Success Story
People with the birth date number eight interact with other people in a businesslike fashion. They are ambitious and confident individuals who are sure of themselves and their ability to succeed in whatever they choose to do. They are respected and admired by others because of their hard work and commitment. They are strong-willed and determined individuals who persevere in the face of adversity.

People with the whole name number eight can become obsessed with material wealth and become greedy and miserly.

Whole Name Number Nine—The Humanitarian
People with the whole name number nine are tolerant, kind and compassionate in their interaction with other people. They are charitable and forgiving individuals who are willing to give anyone a second chance. Other people's opinions are important to them, and they rarely take any form of action without consulting someone else first. They pursue equality and harmony in their lives and are accepting of everyone's uniqueness.

People with the whole name number nine may find it hard

to accept that life is not perfect. They may become disillusioned and frustrated by the lack of harmony in the world.

Name Chart

The use of a name chart helps to reveal more evidence about the influence that your name has on your character. The name chart reflects the strengths and weaknesses that may exist in your personality.

The name chart is a grid exactly like the one used to calculate your birth chart. The numerical value of each letter that appears in your name is placed each time it appears in the appropriate section of the grid (see name chart figure 65).

3	6	9
2	5	8
1	4	7

To find the numbers that relate to the letters in your name, we use the chart that shows which numbers correspond with the letters of the alphabet.

1	2	3	4	5	6	7	8	9
A	B	C	D	E	F	G	H	I
J	K	L	M	N	O	P	Q	R
S	T	U	V	W	X	Y	Z	

To find your name chart, simply follow the steps listed below:
Step 1: Write out the name that you have chosen to work with. If working with the full name, it can be interesting to

work out the name chart for your first name alone before adding in your surname and take note of the difference your surname makes to your reading of your character.

Example: CAROLINE MACDONALD

Step 2: Place the appropriate numbers above the vowels and below the consonants.

Example:

1 6 9 5 1 6 1
CAROLINE MACDONALD
3 9 3 5 4 3 4 5 3 4

Step 3: Record the numbers in the empty grid (figure 66).

Example: (figure 67)

33 33	66	99
	55 5	
11	44 4	

Significance can be drawn from complete and incomplete lines in your name chart. These lines are known as the Arrows of Pythagoras and reflect strengths and weakness in your personality.

1–5–9 The Line of Determination (figure 68)

The presence of this complete number line in a birth chart indicates resoluteness, persistence, dedication, strong will, tenacity, firmness of purpose, conviction, fortitude and stamina.

1–5–9 missing The Line of Resignation (figure 69)

The lack of any numbers present in this line indicates lack of motivation, submission, lack of enthusiasm, unwillingness, lack of determination and lack of originality.

3–5–7 The Line of Compassion (figure 70)

The presence of this line in a birth chart indicates sympathy, consideration, humanity, kindness, understanding, benevolence and intuition.

3–5–7 missing The Line of Scepticism (figure 71)

The lack of any numbers present in this line indicates, lack of trust, suspicion, disbelief, incredulity and cynicism.

3–6–9 Line of the Intellect (figure 72)

The presence of this line in a birth chart indicates intelligence, creative thought, the ability to solve problems and mental agility.

3–6–9 missing The Line of Eccentricity (figure 73)

The lack of any numbers present in this line indicates unconventional thought, nonconformity, lack of logic and individuality.

2–5–8 The Line of Emotion (figure 74)

The presence of this line in a birth chart indicates sensitivity, spirituality, balance, harmony, calm and love.

2–5–8 missing The Line of Sensitivity (figure 75)

The lack of any numbers present in this line indicates a lack of self-confidence, shyness, a sense of inferiority, a tendency to be oversensitive and a tendency to be introverted.

1–4–7 The Line of Physicality (figure 76)

The presence of this line in a birth chart indicates good health, manual dexterity, action, skill, practicality and ability.

1–4–7 missing The Line of Illusion (figure 77)

The lack of any numbers present in this line indicates insecurity, weakness, uncertainty, a tendency to be accident-prone, a lack of practicality and a non-materialistic approach to life.

1–2–3 The Line of the Planner (figure 78)

The presence of this line in a birth chart indicates consideration, neatness, administrative skills, organizational abilities and leadership qualities.

1–2–3 missing The Line of Confusion (figure 79)

The lack of any numbers present in this line indicates disorder, chaos, a lack of balance, muddle and disorganization.

4–5–6 The Line of Will (figure 80)

The presence of this line in a birth chart indicates ambition, determination, single-mindedness, clarity of purpose and sense of direction.

4–5–6 missing The Line of Frustration (figure 81)

The lack of any numbers present in this line indicates a lack of fulfilment, dissatisfaction, disappointment, discontent, resentment and a lack of success.

7–8–9 The Line of Action (figure 82)

The presence of this line in a birth chart indicates enthusiasm, zeal, energy, vitality, power, activity and decisiveness.

7–8–9 missing The Line of Inertia (figure 83)

The lack of any numbers present in this line indicates inactivity, stagnation, passivity, idleness and contemplation.

Intensity Numbers

Intensity numbers are numbers that dominate your name chart. Any number that occurs more frequently than any other in your name chart is known as the intensity number. The intensity number reveals your hidden character and aspects of your personality that are not immediately obvious from the initial analysis of your name. The intensity number is not of primary significance in the analysis of your character through numerology but adds further information.

If there is one number that is dominant in your chart, your intensity number is quite strong. If more than one number is dominant then the effect of the intensity number is weakened.

In the example that we used (see name chart figure 67, page 152) the number three is dominant in the chart. Therefore, Caroline Macdonald has the intensity number three. Three is the number that appears more frequently than any other so the intensity number is quite significant in the analysis of her character.

Below are listed the traits and characteristics associated with each intensity number:

Intensity Number One
Self-aware, strong-willed, assertive, original, confident, able to take control and self-reliant.

Intensity Number Two
Diplomatic, cooperative, thoughtful, considerate, tactful, able to negotiate and compromise, sensitive and noncompetitive, listens to the views of others.

Intensity Number Three
Happy, confident, entertaining, creative, sociable, joyous, optimistic and gregarious.

Intensity Number Four
Practical, traditional, conservative, organized, efficient, hard-working, committed, patient, focused and determined.

Intensity Number Five
Independent, free-spirit, versatile, adaptable, open-minded, skilled in communicating, open to new experiences and change and fond of travel.

Intensity Number Six
Sensitive, balanced, responsible, protective, just, creative, home builder, harmonious, caring, loving and nurturing.

Intensity Number Seven
Loner, thinker, independent, solitary, mysterious, creative, philosophical, observant, secretive, self-contained, content and self-reliant.

Intensity Number Eight
Efficient, ambitious, successful, powerful, determined, wealthy, strong-willed, organized, responsible, trustworthy and dependable.

Intensity Number Nine
Tolerant, compassionate, open-minded, non-judgmental, emotional, sensitive, caring, loving, romantic, idealistic and humanitarian.

Missing Numbers

Missing numbers are sometimes referred to as karmic numbers. They represent qualities that you naturally lack in your personality. They are called karmic numbers because some numerologists believe that your purpose in life is to develop these qualities to achieve happiness and balance.

In this book so far we have looked at various numbers that influence your character: the birth date number, the vowel number, the consonant number, the full name number and the intensity number. To find your missing number, you must record all these numbers and see which numbers from one to nine are not represented.

The example below shows the final set of numbers for Caroline Macdonald born 27.08.1965.

Birth Date Number—2

First Name Vowel Number—3

Surname Vowel Number—8

Full Name Vowel Number—2

First Name Consonant Number—2

Surname Consonant Number—5

Full Name Consonant Number—7

First Name Whole Name Number—5

Surname Whole Name Number—4

Full Name Whole Name Number—9

Intensity Number—3

These are the most significant numbers but to find missing numbers we must also compare the birth chart and the name chart.

Example:

Name Chart (figure 84)

3 3 3	6 6	9 9
	5 5 5	
1 1	4 4 4	

Birth Chart (figure 85)

	6	9
2	5	8
1		7

It can be seen from the two charts that Caroline does not have any missing numbers but the numbers that are represented in the charts alone represent weaker aspects of her character that could be developed.

There is space below for you to fill in the final set of numbers for your name and date of birth.

Birth Date Number—
First Name Vowel Number—
Surname Vowel Number—
Full Name Vowel Number—
First Name Consonant Number—
Surname Consonant Number—
Full Name Consonant Number—
First Name Whole Name Number—
Surname Whole Name Number—
Full Name Whole Name Number—
Intensity Number—
Name Chart (figure 86)
Birth Chart (figure 87)

figure 86

figure 87

If after the final analysis you find that there is one or more numbers that are not represented then you have a missing number. The significance of missing numbers is examined below.

Missing Number One
People who are missing number one from their numerological make-up lack the ability to take the lead and have difficulty in getting themselves heard. They find it difficult to be assertive and are not confident about giving their opinion on matters.

   People who are missing number one should try to build up their self-confidence and take more chances in life.

Missing Number Two
People who are missing number two from their numerological make-up tend to lack the ability to cooperate with other people. They often find it difficult to listen to other people's opinions and ideas and are usually convinced that their position is the correct one to take. They frequently find it difficult to see the opportunity for compromise when they are involved in disputes.

   People who are missing number two should try to hear what other people are saying and should try to be less stubborn.

Missing Number Three
People who are missing number three from their numerological make-up lack the ability to communicate effectively

with other people. They often find that they are not able to express themselves in the way that they would like to. They frequently find that they are misunderstood by other people because of their inability to say what they mean. They tend to have a rather pessimistic view of life and generally have the expectation that things will go against them.

People who are missing number three should try to adopt a more optimistic approach to life and be more open in their interaction with other people.

Missing Number Four

People who are missing number four from their numerological make-up lack order and control in their lives. They tend to float along through life without self-restraint and often end up in financial difficulties. They often have no concept of structure and find it difficult to fit into a working environment.

People who are missing number four should try to be more organized in their daily lives and to practise more self-control. They could also benefit from acting less impulsively.

Missing Number Five

People who are missing number five from their numerological make-up lack the ability to accept change. They tend to live closed lives and are often reluctant to widen their horizons or incorporate new experiences into their lives. They are generally set in their ways and are frequently suspicious of people who have unorthodox lifestyles.

People who are missing number five often find that they become stuck in a rut because of their fear of change. In order to avoid stagnation in their lives they should occasionally make conscious efforts to embrace change. They should try to have an optimistic outlook and not regard change as something that will cause them grief.

Missing Number Six

People who are missing number six from their numerological make-up lack the ability to empathize with other people. They are often rather self-centred individuals who do not always take other people's thoughts and feelings into consideration. They generally dislike responsibility and like to live their lives for themselves. They sometimes have difficulty in expressing their emotions to the people closest to them.

People who are missing number six should try to be more considerate of other people and not always assume that their own needs have highest priority.

Missing Number Seven

People who are missing number seven from their numerological make-up lack the ability to spend time alone with their thoughts. They are often very active people who spend most of their time in the company of other people. They generally live very hectic lives and do not usually allow themselves time to stop and reflect on their actions. They sometimes are overly concerned with material wealth.

People who are missing number seven should try to slow

down and take time to think about their lives. They should try to be less concerned with material gains and should turn their attention to expanding their minds.

Missing Number Eight

People who are missing number eight from their numerological make-up lack any sort of business sense. They are generally lacking in organizational skills and are frequently inefficient individuals who lack motivation and ambition. They tend to be easily put off any course of action by the slightest obstacle in their way.

People who are missing number eight should think about what they want from life and how they can achieve the goals they set themselves. They should try to be more determined to achieve their goals and should not give in so easily.

Missing Number Nine

People who are missing number nine from their numerological make-up lack vision. They tend to be rather narrow-minded and often live sheltered lives. They generally disapprove of lifestyles different from their own. They often lack compassion and tend to have no real interest in the wellbeing of others. Their outlook on life is generally pessimistic and they do not expect much from life.

People who are missing number nine should try to be more open-minded and should not be too judgmental of other people. They should try to understand other people better and look for common ground rather than focusing on differences.

Choosing a Name

Choosing a name for a child or pet is something that people spend a great deal of time thinking about. Numerologists believe that by calculating the number associated with the name being considered, the people choosing a name can determine whether the name is appropriate or not. This section looks at the characteristics associated with each number and gives examples of names.

When choosing a name it is best first to establish the birth date number and then decide on a complementary name number, i.e. you should choose a name that has a name number indicating characteristics that will not cause conflict with the birth date number.

Name Numbers

Number One
Confident—assertive—independent—strong-willed—original—determined—pioneering—powerful—innovative.

Adam	Dan	Jayne	Monica
Agnes	Edith	Joanna	Natasha
Alan	Emily	Juan	Nicolas
Barry	Erin	Kate	Pablo

Bob	Edith	Kay	Rebecca
Bobby	Haleb	Lois	Ralph
Cilla	Hannah	Loren	Tessa
Cindy	Ivor	Lorne	Tyne
Claude	Jackson	Lynus	Zara
Clarissa	Jamal	Mae	Zoe

Number Two
Cooperative—diplomatic—friendly—kind—supportive—calm—understanding—quiet

Adrian	Dennis	Jaclyn	Page
Andrew	Desmond	Jamie	Paulo
Andria	Dianne	Jarrett	Sadie
Ann	Gail	John	Sarah
Asha	Glen	Loyd	Stefan
Dana	Hatty	Nadia	Tony
Denise	Jade	Oscar	Ursula

Number Three
Creative—joyful—charming—communicative—expressive—open—lively—fun-loving

Alec	Clare	Jessica	Natal
Alun	Eamon	Joe	Raja
Amber	Ella	Jock	Sara
Amos	Ellen	Julie	Sasha
Amy	Isabel	Mandy	Scot

Angel	James	Marcus	Sean
Anna	Jane	Mary	Tom
Austin	Jasmin	Mel	Wallace
Celia	Jean	Nancy	Zelda

Number Four
Practical—self-disciplined—stable—hard-working—organized—efficient

Abdul	Clint	Gill	Nathan
Albert	Daisy	Graeme	Neil
Allan	Danny	Hamish	Tracey
Angela	Delia	Harold	Wilma
Annabel	Emmett	Haydon	Winona
Anthea			
Carol			

Number Five
Carefree—curious—communicative—versatile—sensual—independent

Aldo	Frank	Joanne	Paul
Blossom	Isla	Joy	Rossalyn
Donald	Janet	June	Scott
Drew	Jason	Lara	Shelley
Eileen	Jenny	Lloyd	Tommy
Emma	Jim	Maureen	Wayne
Euan			

Number Six

Harmonious—creative—responsible—domestic—loving—caring—sensitive

Ailsa	Dane	Isaac	Lesley
Alex	Diane	Janice	Lydia
Andre	Dougal	Jasper	Malcolm
Arden	Fred	Jered	Maria
Billy	Gary	Joel	Petra
Blair	Grant	Judy	Rae
Bryan	Ian	Karl	Sally
Camilla	Ina	Kim	Selina
Claudia			
Cybil			

Number Seven

Refined—quiet—individualistic—intuitive—thoughtful—contemplative

Amanda	Cassandra	Grace	Sheena
Amon	Chloe	Hazel	Simon
Andrea	Douglas	Isabella	Sinead
Anne	Ewan	Jill	Stewart
Ashley	Flora	Jodie	Todd
Basil	Freda	Lilly	Trudy
Bonny	Giles	Lynne	Walter
Brad	Glenn	Mark	Wanda
Carl			
Carmel			

Number Eight

Powerful—independent—ambitious,—organized—successful—authoritative

Abraham	Colette	Heidi	Laura
Alicia	Colin	Helen	Leah
Alistair	Cynthia	Hugh	Liam
Allen	Danielle	Isobel	Ray
Bernard	Deborah	Jeanette	Ross
Bill	Dudley	Julia	Tina
Brian	Gaby	Justine	Samuel
Carla	Gerard	Keith	Toby
Clara			

Number Nine

Compassionate—idealistic—dramatic—romantic—wise—
caring—empathetic

Alastair	Daniel	Fiona	Roger
Anita	Debbie	Holly	Sandy
Beatrice	Deirdre	Matthew	Sheila
Betty	Dick	Mick	Shelley
Bret	Eddie	Morag	Tiffany
Carmen	Eliott	Nicola	Valerie
Carrie	Erica	Patsy	Vicki
Catriona	Ernest	Reilly	Willy

Numerology and Health

Your birth date number is the most significant number in your life and has the greatest influence over your destiny. Some numerol-ogists have found that there is a connection between your birth date number and your health. They claim that each birth date number is linked to a planet and that each planet rules a certain part of the body. The belief is that people with a certain birth date number will experience health problems associated with the planet that their birth date number is linked with.

This chapter lists the planets that birth date numbers are linked with and the more common health problems that people with these are meant to be susceptible to. This chapter will also look at alternative remedies to the listed health complaints, concentrating on: general action to be taken, diet, herbalism, aromatherapy and dietary supplements. Remember that taking too many vitamin and mineral supplements can be harmful. The advice given is very brief and anyone seriously wishing to use alternative medicine should consult a recognized practitioner.

Birth Date Number One
The Sun

The Sun rules the heart and circulatory system, and Number Ones are prone to illness associated with these. Number Ones may find that they suffer from heart disease, high blood pressure, etc. Lifestyle is very important in the maintaining of a healthy heart, and there is a great deal that can be done to avoid heart problems.

Action

Aerobic exercise is vital to strengthen the muscle of the heart and improve the flow of circulation of blood. It is not necessary to exercise strenuously but exercise that increases the heart rate should be taken on a daily basis. Aerobic activities include walking briskly, swimming, jogging, cycling, skipping and any exercise that increases the heart rate.

For people who have not been used to taking exercise it is important to begin exercising gradually. If there are any concerns relating to health it is advisable to consult a medical practitioner prior to beginning an exercise programme. Many fitness centres and gyms have qualified staff who will be able to conduct fitness tests and give advice on suitable exercises.

Stress is a major factor in many heart complaints, and it is important to relax. Yoga and tai chi are excellent forms of exercise that promote physical and spiritual wellbeing.

Smoking and drinking are major contributors to heart disease.

Diet

Avoid/cut down on:	Include:
saturated fats	fresh, steamed vegetables
sugar	pulses
red meat	nuts
milk	seeds
cheese	fresh fruit
cream	fish
refined and processed foods	tofu
salt	corn
wheat	buckwheat
alcohol	millet
coffee and other caffeine drinks	yoghurt
	honey

Herbal remedies:

Buckwheat tea drunk regularly has a beneficial effect on the circulatory system.

Raspberry leaf tea and ginger root tea have beneficial effects on the heart.

Garlic is excellent for the circulation and should be taken in tablet or capsule form or eaten raw on a daily basis.

Ginseng is good for alleviating stress and should be taken by Number Ones who find relaxation difficult.

Aromatherapy

Number Ones are susceptible to depression and stress. The following essential oils have an antidepressant function and are useful for reducing stress:

bergamot	camomile
clary sage	jasmine
lavender	neroli
rose	

Number Ones have a risk of developing a heart complaint at some time in their lives. The following essential oils are said to help strengthen the muscles of the heart:

lavender	melissa
neroli	ylang ylang

For the circulation problems that Number Ones might encounter the following essential oils are effective in increasing the flow of blood:

juniper	marjoram
rosemary	

These oils can be used in a variety of ways. One option is to apply them through massage by diluting the oils in a carrier oil such as almond or jojoba oil. Another is to place a few drops of oil in a warm bath. Oils can be diluted in a carrier oil or vodka prior to adding them to a bath to avoid irritation. Oils can also be burned in an oil burner.

Supplements

Taking the following vitamins should help to prevent

Number Ones from suffering from the ailments to which they are prone:

calcium	magnesium
vitamin C	vitamin A
vitamin E	

Birth Date Number Two
The Moon

The moon rules the digestive system and the stomach. Number Twos are likely to experience health problems relating to these areas, such as indigestion, flatulence, constipation and diarrhoea.

Action

Many digestive disorders are caused by eating while stressed. Practising relaxation exercises fifteen minutes prior to eating should have a beneficial effect on Number Twos experiencing digestive complaints. Number Twos should ensure that they sit down to eat in an environment without disruptions.

Number Twos should avoid eating large meals late in the day. It is better to eat small amounts of food on a regular basis rather than large amounts at one sitting.

Meals that consist of many different food types put a great deal of stress on the digestive system, and it is better to eat two or three different foods in the course of one meal.

Diet

Avoid/cut down on:	Include:
fatty/greasy foods	whole-grain products
starchy foods	millet
wheat	corn
red meat	buckwheat
shellfish	poultry
cheese	seeds
milk	nuts
sugar	fish
raw vegetables	pulses
tomatoes	yoghurt
citrus fruits	steamed vegetables
coffee	herbal teas
alcohol	

Herbal remedies

Herbal teas are beneficial in the treatment of digestive complaints and should be taken on a regular basis. Spearmint, fennel, camomile, peppermint, comfrey and ginger teas are all noted for their calming effects on the digestive system.

Thyme, oregano, dill, fennel and basil used in cooking will also aid digestion.

Aromatherapy

Number Twos are particularly susceptible to digestive complaints.

For the treatment of diarrhoea the following oils are beneficial:

camomile	cypress
eucalyptus	lavender
neroli	peppermint

The following oils are beneficial in treating constipation:

marjoram	rosemary

In the treatment of flatulence the following oils are particularly effective:

bergamot	camomile
caraway	cinnamon
fennel	ginger
lemon	marjoram
peppermint	rosemary

Because of their soothing qualities the following oils are particularly useful for treating an upset digestive system:

camomile	lavender
marjoram	

These oils can be used in a variety of ways. One option is to apply them through massage by diluting the oils in a carrier oil such as almond or jojoba oil. Massaging the stomach area is particularly useful in the treatment of digestive disorders. Another option is to place a few drops of oil in a warm bath. Oils can be diluted in a carrier oil or vodka prior to adding them to a bath to avoid irritation. Oils can also be burned in an oil burner.

Supplements
The following food supplements are of use to Number Twos:

aloe vera juice   lactobacillus
vitamin B

Birth Date Number Three
Jupiter
Jupiter rules the liver. Number Threes are likely to suffer from health complaints relating to the liver, such as nausea, inertia, constipation, headaches and minor skin complaints.

Action
Liver problems are often the result of excessive strain being put on the liver by consuming large amounts of toxins that need to be eliminated. Number Threes should reduce their intake of toxins such as alcohol, drugs, additives, preservatives and other chemicals.

Diet
Diet is extremely important in the maintaining of a healthy liver.

Avoid/cut down on:	Include:
saturated fats	starchy foods
red meat	grapes
poultry	lemon juice
fish	mineral water
butter	vegetable juices (especially

milk	beetroot and radish
salt	soya milk
sugar	cottage cheese
tea	nuts
coffee	seeds
alcohol	yoghurt
orange juice	honey
oranges	dandelion coffee / tea
	herbal teas

Aromatherapy

The following essential oils help to alleviate the problem of excessive toxins in the body:

Rosemary promotes the production and flow of bile.

Camomile and peppermint are generally beneficial for the liver.

Cypress, lemon and thyme are useful for a congested liver.

Juniper oil also aids the elimination of toxins.

These oils can be used in a variety of ways. One option is to apply them through massage by diluting the oils in a carrier oil such as almond or jojoba oil. Another is to place a few drops of oil in a warm bath. Oils can be diluted in a carrier oil or vodka prior to adding them to a bath to avoid irritation. Oils can also be burned in an oil burner.

Birth Date Number Four
Uranus
Uranus rules the mind. Number Fours may experience minor mental health problems such as melancholia and mild bouts of depression.

Action
Number Fours should keep a mood diary, detailing their moods and actions, to see if there is any connection between certain activities and their moods.

Exercise is beneficial both physically and spiritually and Number Fours should find a form of exercise that they enjoy. Exercise lifts the spirits draws attention away from potentially stressful events and experiences.

It is important for Number Fours to allow themselves time to relax, and they should experiment with different relaxation techniques such as breathing exercises. Yoga and tai chi may also prove to be very helpful.

If they experience a bout of depression that is persistent or overpowering, Number Fours should consider the various forms of therapy available rather than attempt to treat it themselves. They should approach a medical practitioner to discuss their illness and the possible alternative treatments.

Diet

Avoid/cut down on:	Include:
alcohol	fresh fruit
caffeine drinks	fresh vegetables

fatty foods	carbohydrates
sugar	
processed and refined foods	

Herbal remedies

Mix the herbs St John's wort, vervain, wild oat, balm and scullcap together. A teaspoonful of this mixture should be infused in a cup of boiling water and drunk. This should be repeated three times, daily.

Aromatherapy

The following essential oils are very useful for Number Fours because of their sedative and antidepressant properties which are particularly effective in treating stress:

camomile	clary sage
lavender	sandalwood
ylang ylang	

The following essential oils are slightly different in that they have uplifting and antidepressant properties:

bergamot	geranium
melissa	rose

Neroli is effective for stressed Number Fours because it reduces anxiety.

The depression felt by many Number Fours may be the result of a lack of confidence, if this is the case then jasmine is an effective essential oil.

These oils can be used in a variety of ways. One option is to apply them through massage by diluting the oils in a carrier oil such as almond or jojoba oil. Massage is particularly beneficial in the treatment of depression and number fours should consider seeing a qualified aromatherapist for treatment. Another option is to place a few drops of oil in a warm bath. Oils can be diluted in a carrier oil or vodka prior to adding them to a bath to avoid irritation. The use of aromatherapy baths is also good for depression as the depressed person is able to take an active role in the therapy. Oils can also be burned in an oil burner.

Birth Date Number Five
Mercury
Mercury rules the central nervous system. Number Fives may suffer from health complaints if they put too much pressure on their central nervous systems. Insomnia is a common complaint for Number Fives.

Action
Insomnia results from an inability to relax and allow oneself to go to sleep. Number Fives should exercise on a regular basis, which will benefit their health generally and help them to cope with stress. Relaxation techniques should be employed by Number Fives. Yoga, tai chi, meditation and breathing exercise all aid relaxation.

Number Fives experiencing insomnia should avoid eating large meals in the evening. It is better to eat small amounts of food regularly throughout the day so that the body does not have to work hard at digesting whilst trying to sleep.

Many cases of insomnia can be relieved by improving the quality of the sleeping environment. It is important to have a comfortable bed with a firm and even mattress and bedclothes that are warm but not too heavy.

Diet

Avoid/cut down on:	Include:
caffeine	herbal teas
sugar	oats
salt	honey

Herbal remedies

Lemon, thyme and dried hops mixed together and placed in a muslin bag attached to the bed post helps to promote sleep. Passionflower and camomile teas aid relaxation and are beneficial in the treatment of insomnia.

Aromatherapy

Aromatherapy is particularly useful in the treatment of insomnia. An aromatherapy bath before bedtime promotes relaxation and encourages sleep. It is important that the bath should be warm but not too hot.

A visit to an aromatherapist for a massage is advisable for Number Fives suffering from insomnia. Massage is excellent for reducing stress and creating a sense of wellbeing. A massage in the evening, close to bedtime, is particularly beneficial.

Burning relaxing oils in an oil burner beside the bed also helps to promote sleep. These oils are helpful in the treatment of insomnia:

lavender	marjoram
camomile	bergamot
neroli	sandalwood
ylang ylang	

These oils can be used in a variety of ways. One option is to apply them through massage by diluting the oils in a carrier oil such as almond or jojoba oil. Another is to place a few drops of oil in a warm bath. Oils can be diluted in a carrier oil or vodka prior to adding them to a bath to avoid irritation. Oils can also be burned in an oil burner. In the treatment of insomnia it is important regularly to vary the oils being used.

Birth Date Number Six
Venus
Venus rules the lumbar region and venous circulation. Number Sixes are generally blessed with good health and experience few health-related problems. In their later years Number Sixes could experience problems with their circulation.

Action
Number Sixes should exercise regularly to maintain

healthy circulation. Aerobic exercise is particularly beneficial for the circulatory system. Aerobic exercise should be taken on a regular basis but does not need to be strenuous. Forms of exercise that are aerobic are walking briskly, swimming, jogging, skipping, rowing, and anything that increases the heart rate. Introducing exercise into everyday life should be done gradually, and it is a good idea to consult a medical practitioner prior to embarking on an exercise regime.

Acupuncture is particularly beneficial for stimulating the circulatory system. Number Sixes suffering from poor circulation may find that acupuncture alleviates their discomfort. Shiatsu and acupressure both stimulate the flow of energy to organs. Number Sixes with circulation problems should investigate the various alternative therapies and remedies available and decide which one best meets their needs.

Diet

Avoid/cut down on:	Include:
butter	whole grain cereals
cheese	millet
milk	corn
wheat	bran
shellfish	potatoes
sugar	beetroot
refined and processed foods	marrow

fruits	squashes
fruit juices	parsnips
salt	garlic
saturated fats	mustard

Spices such as cumin, cayenne, ginger, curry, coriander, turmeric, etc are helpful to the diet of Number Sixes.

Herbal remedies

Ginger root tea has beneficial effects on the circulatory system, as does buckwheat tea, dandelion tea and coffee.

Garlic taken either in tablet and capsule form or eaten raw on a daily basis will aid circulation.

For poor circulation to the feet, immerse feet in a warm foot bath containing mustard powder.

Aromatherapy

For the circulation problems from which typical Number Sixes suffer the following essential oils are particularly effective in giving some relief:

juniper	marjoram
lavender	ylang ylang
cypress	

These oils can be used in a variety of ways. One option is to apply them through massage by diluting the oils in a carrier oil such as almond or jojoba oil. Massaging hands and feet with the appropriate oils is particularly beneficial if Number Sixes are suffering from poor circulation. Another option is to place a few drops of oil in a warm bath.

Oils can be diluted in a carrier oil or vodka prior to adding them to a bath to avoid irritation. Oils can also be burned in an oil burner.

Supplements
The following supplements are of use to Number Sevens:

magnesium	iron
zinc	flaxseed oil

Birth Date Number Seven
Neptune
Neptune rules the mind and nervous system. Number Sevens tend to be prone to emotional problems that often manifest themselves as skin complaints.

Action
Number Sevens should avoid using heavily scented products that may irritate their skin. They should keep a list of any products that cause an allergic reaction.

Number Sevens should find a method of relaxation that suits them. They should experiment with yoga, tai chi, breathing exercises, meditation, etc, until they find an activity that helps them to relax.

Sunlight is good for the skin, as is outdoor life generally. Number Sixes should ensure that they wear adequate skin protection when out in the sun. Exercising outside helps to eliminate toxins through the skin.

Bathing in a bath containing a half-cup of salt and

half-cup of baking soda is also reputed to help soothe the skin.

Diet
Number Sevens suffering from skin disorders should make note of any foods that causes an allergic reaction and eliminate these from their diet.

Avoid/cut down on:	Include:
tea	fresh, raw vegetables
coffee	steamed vegetables
red meat	whole grains
additives	millet
citrus fruits	buckwheat
chocolate	corn
sugar	cold pressed oils
salt	tofu
tomatoes	pulses
dairy products	seeds
vinegar	yoghurt
shellfish	
wheat	

Herbal remedies
A compress of comfrey and dandelion leaves can be applied directly to areas of irritated skin.
Sasperilla root tea helps skin problems.

Aromatherapy

Bergamot, lavender and sandalwood oils all help skin problems and promote relaxation.

Number Sevens should be careful when using aromatherapy oils and should be aware of any allergic reactions.

These oils can be used in a variety of ways. One option is to apply them through massage by diluting the oils in a carrier oil such as almond or jojoba oil. Massage is particularly beneficial for Number Sevens who are feeling despondent or stressed as it is good for lifting depression. Another option is to place a few drops of oil in a warm bath. Oils can be diluted in a carrier oil or vodka prior to adding them to a bath to avoid irritation. Oils can also be burned in an oil burner.

Supplements

The following dietary supplements are beneficial to Number Sevens:

evening primrose oil	vitamin C
vitamin A	vitamin B
vitamin E	potassium

Birth Date Number Eight
Saturn

Saturn rules the skeleton. Number Eights tend to suffer from headaches.

Action

Number Eights suffering from headaches should keep a diary of when headaches occur and list any possible triggers.

Many headaches are caused by stress and Number Eights should find ways of relaxing and getting rest.

Exercise, especially yoga and tai chi, could prove to be useful in relieving headaches.

Massage to the head, around the temples, can be very soothing for Number Eights suffering from headaches.

Diet

Avoid/cut down on:	Include:
alcohol	fresh fruit
preservatives and additives	fresh vegetables
processed and refined foods	mineral water
caffeine drinks	herbal teas
tobacco	
chemicals	
red meat and animal fats	
dairy products	

Herbal remedies

Many herbal teas help to soothe headaches. Spearmint, camomile, comfrey, raspberry leaf and nettle are all good.

Aromatherapy

The following oils are effective in soothing the headaches to which Number Eights are susceptible:

camomile	rose
lavender	peppermint
rosemary	eucalyptus

The above oils can be diluted by a carrier oil and rubbed directly onto the temples to relieve a headache. Lavender oil does not need to be diluted and can be used alone.

These oils can be applied through massage by diluting them in a carrier oil such as almond or jojoba oil. Alternatively, a few drops of oil diluted in a carrier oil or vodka added to a bath is an effective method. Oils can also be burned in an oil burner.

Supplements
Vitamin B12, potassium and magnesium are effective dietary supplements

Birth Date Number Nine
Mars
Mars rules many parts of the body such as the muscular system, kidneys, urogenital system, etc. Because Mars controls so many areas of the body, Number Nines are often prone to being infected by contagious diseases. Number Nines should maintain a healthy immune system to fight off infection.

Action
Number Nines should aid their bodies to eliminate toxins by keeping fit and healthy by exercising, taking saunas and eating the right foods. Number Nines should also experiment

with meditation and massage to benefit the body as a whole.

Diet

Avoid/cut down on:	Include:
preservatives and additives	yoghurt
caffeine drinks	fish
sugar	eggs
chocolate	tofu
animal fats	carrots
red meat	poultry
dairy products	brown rice
wheat	millet
shellfish	buckwheat
beans vinegar	barley
tomatoes	oats
citrus fruits	leafy, green vegetables
sour fruit	potatoes
	broccoli
	bananas
	melon

Herbal remedies
Camomile tea should be taken in place of caffeine drinks.

Aromatherapy
Number Nines are susceptible to bacteria and viruses. The following oils help to combat this and stimulate the immune system:

lavender	bergamot
eucalyptus	rosemary
niaouli	tea tree

These oils can be used in a variety of ways. One option is to apply them through massage by diluting the oils in a carrier oil such as almond or jojoba oil. Another is to place a few drops of oil in a warm bath. Oils can be diluted in a carrier oil or vodka prior to adding them to a bath to avoid irritation. Oils can also be burned in an oil burner.

Supplements

There are several dietary supplements that are beneficial to number nines:

aloe vera juice	acidophilus
garlic	vitamin C
potassium	magnesium
iron	vitamin B12

Bibliography

Andrews, Ted. *The Sacred Power in Your Name*; Llewellyn Publications, 1990

Anderson, Mary. *The Secret Power of Numbers*, Aquarian Press, 1979

Arcarti, Kristyna. *Numerology for Beginners*, Hodder & Stoughton, 1993

Bek, Lilla & Holden, Robert. *What Number are You?*, Aquarian Press, 1992

Bishop, Barbara, J. *Numerology: The Universal Vibrations of Numbers*, Llewellyn Publications, 1990

Bosman, Leonard. *The Meaning and Philosophy of Numbers*, Rider & Co., 1932

Coates, Austin. *Numerology*, Granada Publishing, 1978

Cole, K. C. *Sympathetic Vibrations*, Bantam Books, 1985

Curtis, Susan; Fraser, Romy and Kohler, Irene. *Neal's Yard Remedies*, Penguin, 1988

Davis, Patricia. *Aromatherapy A–Z*, The C. W. Daniel Co. Ltd, 1988

Duff, Gail. *Country Wisdom*, Pan Books, 1979

Fitzgerald, Arlene, J. *Numbers for Lovers*, Manor Books. 1974

Gibson, Wallace. *The Science of Numerology*, George Sully & Co., 1927

Goodman, Morris, C. *Modern Numerology*, Fleet Press Corporation, 1945

Guthrie, Kenneth. *Sylvan—The Pythagorean Sourcebook and Library*, Planes Press, 1985

Hitchcock, Helyn. *Helping Yourself with Numerology*, Wolfe Publications Ltd, 1972

Kiley, Shirlee & Gordon, Rochelle. *Your Name is Your Destiny*, Pan Books, 1984

Lingerman, Hal. *The Book of Numerology, Taking a Count of Your Life*, Samuel Weiser Inc., 1994

Lingerman, Hal. *Living Your Destiny*, Samuel Weiser Inc., 1992

Oliver, George. *The Pythagorean Triangle*, Wizards Bookshelf, 1975

Rodrigo, Paul. *The Numerology Handbook*, Quantum, 1996

Shine, Norman. *Numerology*, Acrum Press, 1994

Starck, Marcia. *The Complete Handbook of Natural Healing*, Llewellyn Publications, 1991

Wannan, Bill. *Bill Wannan's Folk Medicine*, Fontana, 1972